*J*ess Eva is a radio and television presenter. She currently co-hosts Triple M's *Moonman in the Morning* alongside Lawrence Mooney, and is a regular on Seven's *The Latest* with Michael Usher. Jess and her partner, Norm, were contestants on Channel 9's *The Block*, and most recently she appeared on *I'm a Celebrity . . . Get Me Out of Here!*

But more importantly Jess is a mum, a fiancé of eight freaking years, and a compulsive fuck-up. (The entire human race is a fuck-up. The more we talk about it the better.) She came last at javelin three years in a row at Tatura Primary School. She slept with numerous men in an attempt to find happiness: it failed. She has the worst bikini line Australia has ever seen and therefore has a phobia about being too close to a naked flame. And now she's writing a book . . . Gee, the world's a funny place.

Why Wouldn't Ya?

JESS EVA

MACMILLAN

Pan Macmillan Australia

First published 2021 in Macmillan by Pan Macmillan Australia Pty Ltd
1 Market Street, Sydney, New South Wales, Australia, 2000

 A catalogue record for this book is available from the National Library of Australia

Typeset in 12.75/19 pt Adobe Garamond Regular by Post Pre-press
Printed by IVE

 The paper in this book is FSC® certified. FSC® promotes environmentally responsible, socially beneficial and economically viable management of the world's forests.

This book is dedicated to anyone who has ever doubted themselves. To anyone who ever thought they weren't good enough. We're going to capture your self-worth, together.

Contents

You have one life: to waste it existing opposed to living is a modern-day tragedy, yet most of us are guilty of this. Today is the day you stop existing and start living.

Introduction

EVERYTHING YOU'VE BEEN THINKING IS WRONG

During this book I need to talk to you personally. You're reading this, so we're already friends, and if we ever meet we NEED to have a wine together. Also, all friends have nicknames, so your nickname is Knackers. Why? Because . . . look, don't question me, Knackers, just keep reading, we've got work to do! (Did we just have our first fight?)

Think of something you want to do right now, and ask yourself: why wouldn't ya? I'm guessing the reasons why you wouldn't dance around the subject of failure. STOP IT, KNACKERS! This is a negative habit you have taught yourself and have spent your entire life practising. So let's take that out. Let's strip away every response you have that surrounds failure or 'what if' or 'but'.

Now, what other reason do you have to not do this? This time your mind may go to some kind of hurdle like family or lack of time. STOP IT! This is your mind trying to self-sabotage you! Fuck off, brain! You have created this excuse – this predefined neurological pathway – for decades; it's normal for your mind to jump on autopilot and fly in self-sabotaging mode. But we need to break that habit NOW. Think about a time you've changed something in your house like, say, where you kept the kitchen bin. After you moved it, it took time, right, to re-train your brain, and stop going back to where the bin used to live? Well, your brain doesn't miraculously work a different way for any other habit. You're letting what you knew and learnt in the past influence your future, which, okay, makes sense in theory. But what if what you knew and learnt in the past was wrong? What if you are creating your future based on past *bad* habits? We need to break those bad habits. And I mean break them. You can't just run away from them.

I once moved to India for enlightenment. Turned out I was every bit as screwed up there as I was here, just in a different geographical location and $1500 poorer from the plane ticket. Yep, your pesky little brain, with all its flaws, will follow you around like a bad smell, no matter where you go. So it doesn't matter where you are, what you're doing, how time poor you are. Do you want a better life? Let's do it together!

Some self-help books tell you that in order to have a purposeful life you need to work on having the perfect relationship, or start your own business, or make a million dollars working two hours a day, three days a week. Which of course never happens, so you feel like a bigger screw up than when you started the book and the only solution seems to be to wallow in your self-misery by eating a jar of gherkins and sucking down a pineapple Vodka Cruiser. But guess what: self-motivation and having a kick-arse life aren't always about having a freaking boyfriend or an ABN or some kind of bullshit mood board. I personally hate crafts, so the thought of achieving a dream by having to cut out stuff from a magazine, glue it onto a piece of poster paper and look at it every day only puts me in the mood to scull a bottle of wine and take my top off. In saying that, hmmm, taking my top off . . . Why wouldn't ya?

So now I'm topless. By myself, with a dog. Why? Because I'm 36 and can do whatever I want. Here, I'll prove it to you and take a webcam shot:

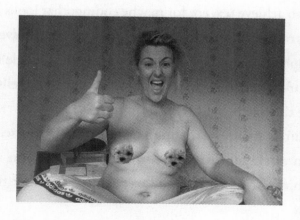

Please note, Knackers: my nipples have been replaced by my dog Denise's face. Just in case you were worried my breasts had developed three black areolas and hair.

Anyway, my point is, I'm 93 kilograms of average-looking white chocolate. If I can sit here topless like some weird uncooked chicken with only my dog for company, I'm sure you can have a crack at doing whatever it is you want to do!

Maybe you just want to experience life at a better level. Maybe you don't want to be held back by the word no. Maybe if you said 'Why wouldn't ya?' to more things you would experience more, and better, things. It's the power of asking yourself, *How do* I *do that?* when you see or hear someone else doing something you'd like to do. It's about seeking the power of 'doing' as opposed to 'wishing'. It doesn't matter where you've come from, what circumstance you are in: the only thing holding you back is your mind. The only person holding you back is *you*! I promise you, Knackers, this is true! You are capable of whatever you want to achieve (except for maybe coding, that looks really hard and very boring to learn). Listen to me! You've seen me topless, I wouldn't lie to you! You are the Google Maps of your own destiny and despite what your mind tells you, you're the one behind the steering wheel.

Your previous habits may make you tell yourself you are an arsehole, that you don't deserve what you aspire to achieve. The world is full of people who think they're arseholes. Every person on the planet has doubted themselves and thought they were not enough. Your kind old neighbour who's always offering you lemons from her tree, your hairdresser who could talk under water, the guy on the street who picks up your groceries when the shopping bag handle shits itself: all of these people have thought they were an arsehole. Our inner narrative is constantly reminding us that we aren't enough, we need to do more, we need to make more money, we need to be kinder to our children, our friends and our partners. But I want you to know, everything you are doing IS enough. It's the story we tell ourselves that is failing. We hunt down the evidence to support our self-hatred and lack of self-worth, yet we dismiss the evidence of everything we are doing right. We rob ourselves blind of our inner worth every day by comparing ourselves to an impossibly perfect life. I call it the 'shoulds'. 'I should be better.' 'I should earn more money.' 'I should have a new house.' 'I should be able to go to the shops without the kids crying.' That life doesn't exist . . . for anyone! You ARE enough, you ARE worth loving and you ARE capable of peace and fulfilment. Unfortunately, you're the last person to realise it. There is scientific evidence that proves we create habits around self-hate, hating others and sabotaging our own lives. But you can stop that now.

The methods I suggest in this book undoubtedly saved my life. They gave me emotional time with my children.

They enhanced the quality of my professional work and allowed me to open myself up to feel love without guilt. In turn, that made me love those around me to a level I never thought possible. And to do that I didn't have to change my job or partner, turn vegan or ring some of those miniature Buddha symbol things fulfilled people tend to clang together. Everything stayed the same; the difference was I was able to create new habits – new neurological pathways – to think positively. (Shit. I hate the phrase 'think positively'. It's what people tell you when you get a terminal cancer diagnosis. But it turns out there is something to it . . .) I was able to give myself relief from the downward spiral of everyday life and maintain a sense of happiness and love for myself and others. Something I never thought possible, and maybe you feel that way too. Maybe you get annoyed at your partner, or constantly feel hard done by; if you have doubted yourself, if you want to lose weight or if there's always something you wanted to do. Can you imagine a life free from over-thinking and self-hate? You can bloody have it! I was able to develop a method that dug me from the emotional trenches and gave me a life where I *live*, rather than just exist. It starts with your head, and until you get that right, how can you celebrate your wins? How can you enjoy the journey that takes you to your goals?

Whatever stress you're feeling, whatever is giving you anxiety, well, today is the day you leave it behind, because you and I have a roadmap of where you need to go. And we are going to start that journey NOW. So pour yourself a glass of wine and let's do this together. Why wouldn't ya love yourself? Why wouldn't ya strive for peace and happiness? Why wouldn't ya emotionally quit toxic people and find your self-worth? Just WHY WOULDN'T YA?

✷

Hellloooooooooo, internal peace and happiness, where are you? I found you last night in a sav blanc bottle at the bowls club after I won a meat raffle (is there any bigger thrill than winning a raffle? I think not). But you quickly disappeared when I overindulged in the glass bottle of happiness and fulfilment, called Norm (my partner of eight years, my one and only, my bald, hairy-balled soulmate on this roller-coaster of life) an arsehole because he wouldn't give me $20 to put on Keno, tried to make an old woman I'd never met, who was minding her own business, sing karaoke with me, when there was no karaoke, just a song in my head and a free microphone sitting on the lawn bowlers' table, and chundered in the bowls club pot plant while walking home.

Next thing I remember was waking with that taste in my mouth like someone had spiked my saliva with dirt, alcohol and syrup. As I reached for my phone to see if anyone had abused me for my reptilian behaviour via text, I reinvested my belief in fate when I saw the head-line on my Apple News notifications: 'THE $40 ITEM THAT CHANGED MY LIFE'. Knowing I had $70 in my account, I was thinking, *This could be it!* My lifetime search for answers was over. Thank the lord, whoever you may be! I reflected on a life of expensive attempts at fulfilment, like the $35 a week for a yoga studio I've never been inside, only to be haunted by reminder texts that they haven't seen me for a while or my payment has bounced. When we can change our lives with a $40 product! Why hadn't the world told us about this earlier? If I'd had this product 24 hours ago, I wouldn't have been facing a day of apologies and grovelling to those I'd insulted at the bowls club.

It must be the bloody pharmaceutical companies! I read in a Byron Bay magazine that they are evil; that they are the reason we are unhealthy and miserable. They hide how easy (and cheap) it is to find happiness because they want to keep us on antidepressants. It wouldn't surprise me if the pharmaceutical companies put the headache in wine, just so we buy their Panadol the next day. Holy shit, I might just be paranoid from the dehydration, but are pharmaceutical companies and wine in it together? Wine has a secret deal to create headaches and nausea that only Panadol can fix?

Come on, alcohol, you've given me and the rest of the world an absolute hiding at times. But we stick with you!

If a partner had hurt me as much as you have, I would have left by now and called the cops. Imagine if my partner had made me crowd surf at a business excellence awards night in 2007, wearing nothing under my boob tube dress, which soon curled up at either end, hugging my waist like a belt, exposing both the love puppies and the nook and cranny. And imagine if I was not 'surfed' but 'bag of spudded' on the floor, leading to a broken ankle and an ambulance call-out. Yeah, well, if my partner had made all of those things happen, they'd have an AVO out on them. But noooooooo, I stuck with you, Savvy B, through thick and thin. I took the blame for you, when people labelled me a 'mess' or when I slept with that guy called Ian who claimed he invented whiteboard paint (how was I to know 'invented whiteboard paint' was code for 'sell meth to children and live at my mum's house'?). I took the blame for all that, Savvy B! No one bags you out, do they? The company wasn't called and told, 'Your wine is turning a young woman into an absolute piss-rate disgrace who believes meth addicts invent whiteboard paint!' No, it was all Jess. So for the sake of our friendship, alcohol, I HOPE you haven't teamed up with the pharmaceutical companies to sell extra Panadol on Sunday mornings.

But back to my Saturday morning. Life had thrown me a bone: the Apple News headline promising 'the $40 item that changed my life!' My fate was only a swipe away.

I would jump on that fad and suck the sweet nectar out of it like a newborn puppy at a mamma's teat. As I clicked on it, the internet ran a little slow but I didn't care. I had been waiting for this for 35 years, waiting as Forrest Gump had waited for Jenny, so I was happy to wait for another 25 seconds of buffering.

The photo under the headline featured a beaming woman, radiating health and life-changing happiness. The article itself started with 'Stacey never felt better, all of her troubles and fears suddenly disappeared.' You ripper, keep it coming, Stacey, what did you do? 'She always suffered from low confidence and didn't believe in herself, but all of a sudden she felt like she could achieve and do anything.' Righto, Stacey, stop with the blabbing, I'm glad you're happy but stop showing off and share the secret, sister! 'That's the day Stacey's life changed.' Yeah we know, we know, two more paragraphs of this crap and my millennial mind would find internal happiness elsewhere because it was taking too long to crack the code. 'Stacey felt on top of the world.' Yep, don't really care what you're on top of, Stace mate. Just tell me how your life changed by $40. 'Stacey felt invincible when she first tried ice.'

The fucking fuckity fuckstick! Are you kidding? ICE! As I scrolled down past Stacey in her activewear looking amazing, I realised it was her 'before' shot. 'After' shot Stacey was glaring at me, teeth missing, scabs on her face like a dot-to-dot drawing. Holding one of those mug shot signs because she robbed her granny with a homemade knife/stick thing and stole 37 bucks. Woooo, Stacey looks like she's having a ball!

But after seeing her toothless scabbed-out persona, I did feel better. Stacey did change my life after all (and for free!). Because although I had abused my partner and forcibly made an innocent lady sing a song that only existed in my head, at least I wasn't Stacey. Should I track her down and thank her? Should I tell her the positive impact she'd had on my life at that moment as I lay in bed, wearing only a bra, with the feeling of a thousand horses pounding inside my skull from the cheap bowls club wine? Flashes of Stacey, in the dead of night, the moonlight glistening off her scabs like pink diamonds as she threatened to stab her grandmother with a blade gaffer-taped to a stick if Granny didn't hand over her coin purse, flooded my thoughts and vision. I opted to do a morning wee instead.

On making it to the kitchen, I looked at Norm and said good morning, awaiting his response so I could analyse his tone like a Russian spy. Don't you hate that? You only get two days in a weekend, so if you screw up on a Friday night, the thought of wasting a Saturday being in trouble is depressing. The thought that the entire universe hates you is only a bonus.

He looked back at me with a smile. 'Morning, Boozy! Coffee?'

Oh my god, had I hit the jackpot? Maybe Norm was BLIND last night and the gods above had granted me a wild card for the weekend by making him black out. That was my best bet here. Come on, Normy, tell me you drank until you blacked out. I went all in on it! 'Do you remember anything from last night?'

'Yeah, you were feral,' he sniggered.

'Are you angry?' I asked, confused.

'Nup, I read a quote yesterday.'

Completely bewildered, I asked him what it was he had magically read. Because until that moment, the only way I'd thought I could get out of the crap basket was if he had met up with Stacey for a $40 glass BBQ breakfast and the buzz of an illicit drug was clouding his judgement.

Now, when I tell you what he said, you should imagine a balding man wearing a pair of jocks with a hole in the left butt cheek, stirring Nescafé into two old stained cups, and pretend he's talking to you. Especially if you've ever had anyone ever say something to you that's ruined your day. You know, when your boss is mean to you at 10 am and when 7 pm hits, nine hours later, you're still talking to your friends or partner about it, at home on your verandah with a wine, getting more and more worked up . . . plotting his or her death or demise etc. Okay, back to the visualisation of a jock-wearing, balding Nescafé maker.

'If you had $86,400 and you lost $10, would you throw the $86,390 away looking for the $10?'

'No.'

'There are 86,400 seconds in a day, and if someone uses ten of those seconds to upset you, why would you lose the rest of those seconds focusing on the ten?'

I looked at Norm and his holey jocks, gobsmacked at the wisdom of a man who's go-to quote is usually 'Fuck 'em' or, if not, something he read off the back of a bottle cap.

But he's right: if you lost the $10 you wouldn't care because you'd still have $86,390! You'd still be rich and could do so much with that cash. If you met a random stranger and you asked how they were and they said, 'I'm terrible! I dropped a tenner this morning so I spent 86 grand today hiring a search party to find the tenner, and we didn't find it so now I have nothing,' you'd think they were mad! Clinically INSANE.

But that's what we do to our mind! We focus on the ten seconds we lost and not the 86,000 plus that we still had. And chances are the person who stole those seconds doesn't even know or care. So why give them more? If a robber took $10 off you, would you reward them by asking for their bank account details and saying, 'Hey mate, I've got another $86,000 . . . here, have the rest . . . I insist!' NO! You would protect the remaining cash you have. You would feel entitled to your own money and adamant that no one can steal that off you. So let's try and take the same ownership of our time (which is a shit ton more valuable).

No grudges, no hang-ups, no love lost. Norm and I aren't going to break up because I called him an arsehole. I feel bad about it and need to learn not to do it again. But by giving each other the silent treatment, resenting one another or becoming defensive, we only lose valuable seconds on earth. So we talk, resolve, learn and live.

Our bank balance of life isn't going to last forever . . . why wouldn't ya want to spend it wisely and keep it all for yourself?

Anyway, I'm financially BROOOOOOKE! On my arse! Living pay cheque to pay cheque – well, pay cheque to the week before my pay cheque and then on my arse again. Which means if I'm emotionally broke, then I've got absolutely nothing. So I'm hoarding those emotional coins like they're rolls of toilet paper in global pandemic. And as much as I'm sure the glass barbie's a shortcut to endorphin city, I think we need another angle on fulfilment.

So that's what this book's about: sharing my journey towards finding some inner peace so that you can hopefully find some too. We'll meet a lot of pricks and arseholes, and sometimes they'll be living inside your own head. But we'll also learn how to cleanse ourselves of these negative influences. We'll talk about failure, because no one nails it the first time. We even talk science. As I've said, the techniques in this book changed my life forever. They changed the lives of people around me. They saved us from wasting our lives on worry and judgement. In this book we are going to learn how to make the most annoying people in the world be less annoying and the meanest people unable to hurt you. You're going to regain your self-control and journey towards your best life, free from the shit that dangles from us every freaking day! Because you have everything you need, you just don't realise it. Don't worry, though, you will. I can't wait to share with you.

Let's go!

1

QUIT THOSE
PRICKS

*W*hat's bothering you right now? *Who's* bothering you right now? Has someone been mean to you or unfairly judged you, and now you can't stop thinking about them? Do you have that feeling in your guts where you can't decide if you should sob until you start blowing snot bubbles or chase someone down with a baseball bat? Do you like that feeling? I'm guessing no, and in this chapter we are going to create the skills that will help you stop that person keeping you up at night.

Why do you need these skills? Because the world is full of pricks. Manipulative pricks, lying pricks, mean pricks and pricks that don't even know they're pricks, though if they knew how much their prick buckets were over-flowing with prickish behaviour, well, they'd probably blame you, call you a name, get you to mop it up with your favourite T-shirt and make you apologise to THEM. Bloody pricks.

You know the worst thing about them? They're like leeches. They suck every piece of energy from you like a six-year-old slurping a McDonald's vanilla thickshake right down to the dregs. They drain you! And they do it in a way that you don't realise the extent of the damage that they're doing. They're in disguise, getting inside you and attacking you from within, like the SAS but this time it's the PAP: Pricks Are Prominent!

Pricks turn you into someone you don't recognise or like. They make you feel negative, worthless, nervous, weird. They make you say things that you normally wouldn't say and be someone you wouldn't normally be. I remember dating a guy who told me how lucky I was to date him, and I felt so inferior I would always end my sentences with 'So yeah, that's rad'. Fucking cringe! But he stripped away my self-worth, so I wasn't even confident enough to end a sentence without falling back into acting like a person that wasn't me. That's how heavy the burden of someone else's insecure or selfish behaviour can be. But you have more chance of giving birth to piglets than changing the other person. Plus why put all of your energy into trying to fix someone else, and making them a better person, when you're struggling? The only way we can flourish in this situation is to change our own heads. Train our minds to strip the pricks' words of all meaning, so it's just noise.

If we don't, the pricks and their prickish behaviour will crowd your thoughts, making you talk or think about them ALL THE TIME! It's like their negativity is a virus that eats away at your frontal lobe. If you work with them, you spend hours bitching about them to your colleagues over wines. If you date them, you take up every FaceTiming moment with friends talking about them to the point where no one can get a word in about anything else. When someone's talking about something else, you will find a segue – 'Oh yeah, that's like *insert prick's name here* . . .' or 'that's not as bad as *insert what prick-face did here* . . .' It ALWAYS comes back to that prick. If you are or have been in this situation, you have been officially pricked. As much as you might say, 'Oh, I'm just getting it off my chest', it's not healthy. Even if you don't talk about them all the time, they are probably dominating your head space. You start to become addicted to the negativity. You start to create habits that only lead in one direction, and it's a bad one. You stop looking for solutions and you fester in the negativity. It becomes an addiction. You develop a negative thought pattern and associate it with everything else in your life, including people and things you love. Just like an addiction, it pops up when you least expect it, leaves a devastating path and ruins your quality of life. And just like any addict, it's not your fault. It's a disease: something or someone is making you do this. And that's the scariest part about it.

Since addicts are usually the last people to admit to having a problem, let's do a little pop quiz to see if you're a prick addict.

- How many people have pissed you off in the past week? Maybe someone annoyed you on Monday, then a different person annoyed you Tuesday and then Monday's annoying person annoyed you again Thursday and Friday. (If more than one person, give yourself a point.)

- How long did you stay pissed off for? (If more than one full day, give yourself a point.)

- When you talk to your friends, do you talk about someone who is currently annoying you, or do you bring up a past situation where someone annoyed you, which makes you feel frustrated again? (If yes to either of these, give yourself a point.)

- Does the way someone looks or acts or smells annoy you? (If yes, give yourself a point.)

Be honest with yourself. Why would you bother to read this book if you aren't going to be honest? We aren't playing with small change here, we are playing with your happiness, fulfilment and success. You might think, *Yes, well, I have been annoyed with that person for a week, but it's fine* or even *I'm not* that *annoyed*. But the tree of negativity starts as a tiny seed, so if you find yourself having to justify or explain your reasoning as to why you shouldn't score a point on a question, it means you need to give yourself a point. If your addiction is still a seedling, you've got onto it early. We can throw some mental weed killer on that prick and undo the habits you've developed. If it's grown like a blackberry bush, overtaking every thought, that's still okay! We have some work to do but we have the tools to dig it out and uproot it.

If you scored even one point to the questions on the previous page, I'm sorry to say you're a prick addict. Consider this your intervention. I'm only doing it because if we met I'd love you! You need to quit pricks now and release yourself.

I once worked with a guy – fortunately not for too long – who would run and tell the general manager everything I did wrong. If I didn't do something wrong, he would make something up. By the time I heard about it through the gossip pipeline of the office, it had usually been exaggerated through Chinese whispers. But at times my boss would question me over things I had no idea about. In hindsight, this prick's self-worth was so low he needed to bring about other people's downfalls, whether they be real or not, just to make himself feel better. He couldn't care less about the way I felt, it was all narcissistically focused on his own self-worth. But I took it personally.

He read my emails and went through Facebook messages left open on my desktop, scrolling through months of private conversations looking for his name and taking anything he found to management. But meanwhile he was very nice to my face. And that's how many pricks play . . . as silent assassins. They make themselves feel important by playing up (or making up) your weaknesses, even if they signal it just with an eye roll or sigh, so they can tell everyone that they have 'saved the day'. The more these pricks get into your head, the more power they hold. Even their slightest sigh will make you want to leapfrog the desk and ninja punch them right in the throat (not that you ever would, but in the moment it's a delicious daydream!).

When I was under this prick's thumb, I felt terrible, like everyone hated me and believed the bad things he was saying about me. I felt apologetic for things I hadn't done because I carried the weight of someone who had done them. I over-analysed every eyebrow raise from co-workers and assumed he'd been in their ear as well. (He probably hadn't, but this was his power over me.)

I started believing my actions had justified the sighs or looks he would give me. How could I not? Between his negative reactions and my reflections on them, I created a narrative in my mind that I wasn't good enough and everyone around me knew it. I was miserable, an empty shell of the person I had once been. I remember that person. The person who was fun at parties, loved by everyone and loved life. The child who believed all was good in the world and refused to think otherwise. Until I learnt otherwise and adapted my train of thought to think the worst. I would lie awake at night replaying conversations in my head that had happened months or years before. It felt so bad at times, I would go to the mirror and just look at myself and say, 'I hate you, I hate you!' However nobody really knew because I would plaster on a smile.

My every waking thought was dominated by this guy. I would be anxious on the way into work about what he would do that day. I would finish work and talk about him to anyone who would listen, but I wasn't really looking for a way out. Like an addict, I just wanted to wallow in the situation. Every problem I had in my life was because of this guy. My career wasn't progressing because he wouldn't let me, my personal life was suffering because he stressed me out so much at work. He was rotting me from the inside out.

Every time this guy did one prickish act, I would replay that act, on average, 100 times, whether through an internal discussion with myself, a thought or a conversation with friends. This sounds like a large number but according to a psychologist in *Forbes* magazine that's the average number of times a negative emotional situation reappears in our conscious mindset. Say you're at the fridge getting some milk and, just as you reach for the carton, a memory of your prickish situation flashes before your eyes. The way it makes you feel becomes exaggerated, your self-worth plummets and every insecurity you have is flooded into your conscious thought like a tsunami. For fuck's sake, you were just trying to put some full-fat dairy in your tea but BOOM: your prick addiction over-loads your day like an out-of-control firecracker . . . day ruined! Or you hear a story of someone similar and it reminds you of that time . . . day ruined! Even a smell that reminds you of that dark place can make it all come crashing back, and before you know it, you've given that one incident so much energy it feels like it's happened to you 100 times. And each time you think about it, it feels worse than the last, because the baggage is carried over.

Let's do the maths. I think this guy would have been prickish MINIMUM once a week. In a standard month that means about four times a month . . . okay, not so bad. But I thought about and re-lived these prickish things 100 times each, so that's 400 times a month. Hmmm, it's starting to add up. Imagine if I stayed there a year, or five years, which is pretty standard for a lot of jobs these days: that's 100 prickish moments a week, times 48 working weeks in a year, times five years, which equals – get this – 24,000 times!

No fricking wonder I was a ball of anxiety who drank every bottle of wine that came within arm's distance and started crying! I'd managed to brainwash myself into being a tortured soul with no escape. *Ahhhhhh . . . hand me another bottle of $5 Savvy B . . . Mamma needs to numb her pain.*

If you've discovered you're a prick addict, like I was, I have good news and bad news for you.

The bad news: pricks don't change so don't even try. You're not the captain of their destructive behaviour. But you're a kind, empathetic person, so in the past you've probably tried to protect a prick from their own bad habits, and I bet they did not thank you for this. Because pricks don't care about your feelings. They will pretend they do, but only so they can boost their own image. Pricks will respond to your concerns with 'I feel terrible you think I would be capable of that' or something similar, basically spinning the empathetic wheel around to righteously be the victim and maintain control of your emotions to once again make you feel bad.

(By the way, if you're ever put in that situation, don't back away from your original argument. Respond with, 'Well, whether you're capable or not, you *have* done this, so we need to address the situation and you can deal with the aftermath in your own time.' Or put it in your own words, but don't ever let them make you apologise for addressing the behaviour. Because if you do . . . sorry, you've been pricked again.)

And don't ever seek a prick's approval! It's like getting a personal reference from a hitman; what is it actually going to do for you? Today, they will make you feel on top of the world with their compliments and tomorrow they will make you feel like the lowest dog in the pack. But you're a nice person, so you will hang in there and wait for the next time they make you feel good about yourself, only to be brought down once more as the destructive cycle continues.

If you accept this for the rest of your life, you're a prick addict. Like a drug addict, you will live for the highs and ride out the lows. You might think this is okay, just like a drug addict does. A drug addict doesn't know why their friends are saying they need to quit the drugs, because they've created a whole bunch of habits to normalise the longing for a high and that's what keeps them going.

Being a prick addict is actually worse than being a drug addict because there's no prick rehab. Your friends and family won't be waiting for you when you get home one night to stage an intervention over the prick in your life. You will normalise the lows and feel like you deserve it. You will start to feel gratitude towards the prick for helping you become a better person. Because after they drag you down, whenever you show a moment of your true self, the prick will make you feel like they created that moment in you (yes, they'll even steal that part!). Which is complete and utter bullshit because you created that moment, baby, no one else – that's yours! But as their prickishness grows, your brilliance will slowly fade. You are still capable of it, but you are being so badly affected by that prick it's impossible to rise above the level of self-doubt they've created in you. If you hadn't come across this book, you might have lived in this negative situation forever, being robbed of a truly fulfilled, happy and successful life. But stick with me, because we are going to learn how to quit them!

*

Are you ready for the good news now?

Half the reason why pricks have such a huge effect on you is because you let them. I don't want to sound like a prick but it's half your fault (even though you didn't mean it). You have been living in an imaginary world where your reality has been altered. You're actually fucking fantastic! And if your mind is strong enough to warp reality and get you thinking everything's going to shit, imagine what it's capable of when we redirect that passion into something positive! Into something you really want to do in life! It's pretty freaking exciting and it's all you, baby. You ARE going to do this and you ARE going to succeed. You are in the driver's seat – we just need to tweak a few things under the hood first so you can use the energy you have been putting into the worry and anxiety of life into reaching your full potential instead.

Not only are you going to have more emotional time to spend with your family, you are going to start doing what you've always wanted to do.

First some housekeeping: EMOTIONALLY QUIT THE PRICKS! I say 'emotionally' because sometimes you can't physically leave them due to work, etc. But also, why should you? You are just going to meet another one at the next place and you can't run forever. It's time to stand up and create the habits to deal with these guys so you can find the fulfilment you deserve.

I want you to think of the person that bothers you the most. How have you improved your life or situation by obsessing about them for hours? Not at all. How many times have you filled your head with someone you don't even like, completely consuming it, leaving no room for your brilliance to flower? Many. How many times have you lost precious and valuable quality time with your friends or loved ones because this person, who you wouldn't even invite around for a friendly drink, has dominated your mind? I'm guessing many, many times!

Now, say 'I quit [their name]' out loud. Break up with their influence on you. Lock your emotional door and reserve the key for those you love. TAKE YOUR POWER BACK RIGHT NOW! No longer will this person control you or the way you think. Say it again: 'I quit you'. If they are in a bad mood, that's *their* shit and it's got nothing to do with you. Stop absorbing other pricks' shit . . . quit it! You are not a shit shoveller for their soul. You are planting the seeds for your own fulfilment. But you can't grow a garden while you're carrying someone else's shit. You see, if your happiness, fulfilment and success was a garden, pricks would be in there spraying insecticide everywhere. They kill everything great about you and won't allow you the freedom to grow. You need to emotionally quit them now and let yourself be free from their dominance.

So whenever they say something to you and you start to feel frustrated or sad . . . remember you've quit them. They no longer exist in your mind. When they play their games and you're about to take the bait . . . remember you've quit them, so don't play back. You don't have time for these games anymore.

Have you emotionally quit them yet? Try breathing in and breathing out. You'll be able to tell when you've quit them because you'll feel lighter when you breathe. Don't let those negative thoughts come through about 'oh, what about when they . . .' or 'but I have to see them on . . .' EMOTIONALLY QUIT THEM! Let's try again. Breathe in and hold it . . . now breathe out. How does that feel? You quit! Give yourself the emotional freedom to be you, without any negative influence.

Every little piece of negativity will be rampaging inside your brain right now, trying to get back into your subconscious. Let's imagine your negative thoughts look like miniature versions of the person you are emotionally quitting. They are pissed off because they've had control of your mind for so long, they are not coping with the eviction notice. Every time you breathe in and out, you can probably feel them trying to get back in like ants to spilled sugar. Squash them, Mortein them, quit them and when they get back in (which they will), toss them away and remind yourself you've quit those little pricks.

There's actually a scientific reason for this negativity. The minute you emotionally quit that person, you created a new way of thinking, which physically means your mind started building a new neurological pathway in the brain to support it. But you have also begun destroying the old prick-addicted way of thinking. That negativity buzzing inside you right now is a bloody stubborn neurological pathway in the brain that is trying not to die. So while at this moment you're in combat with your old and new ways of thinking, here's how to make sure the new one wins.

Just like a mother wants to protect a child growing inside her, you're now growing a new pathway that will change your life, and protecting that pathway is what you need to focus on. It is vulnerable and needs your care to survive. You care for it by feeding it; you feed it by blocking the old habit of negativity and substituting it with positivity. The negativity is like a disease trying to kill the new life form, but you must do everything in your power to protect it. The pathway will grow stronger with repetition until the positive behaviour is the new normal. It is estimated that it takes 10,000 repetitions to master a habit and develop the associated neural pathway, which on average takes around 30–66 days. But each day will get easier as the pathway gets stronger. Your job is to interrupt your old thoughts and patterns when they arise. This applies not only to pricks, but also to any habit or mindset shift you are looking to achieve.

Once you've emotionally quit the pricks in your life and are actively working on exterminating the negative thoughts that have controlled you for so long, you will no longer be someone's puppet. The puppet show will be completely in your hands. What will your show be about?

So let's grow the fuck out of those damaging pathways together. Let's do it again: breathe in . . . breathe out . . . and say 'I quit you' . . . breathe in again and this time breathe out the energy that has been bottled up inside you. Was it a little easier that time?

I want to be the first to congratulate you, because you just released yourself from someone who has been dimming your light for a while! If I was with you I would crack a bottle of bubbly and celebrate. You still have a lot of work to do, but you have now freed up so much of your mind and your energy to focus on your true path and the people who deserve your time. Feel empowered? You should!

When we emotionally quit negative people, we are actually changing ourselves. As I said earlier, pricks don't change but you can. You were tangled in a web of energy-draining pricks, and now, thank goodness, you're free, creating new pathways to your better life. You know the interesting part? The more you emotionally quit situations, the less analysing and overthinking you do, and funnily enough you become better. You become a better partner, mum, dad, colleague . . . you become better all round! You have let go of everything that was holding you back from your brilliance and that is the over-thinking, anxiety and doubt. You will still have small pricks inside you (pardon the pun) but those are just the negative thoughts. Quit those pricks too. The thought that you're going to screw up? Quit that prick. Just focus on what you can control and that is what you do and *solely* what you do. QUIT ALL THE PRICKS RIGHT NOW . . . do I need to make you breathe again? Okay, you've got it! (But seriously, one more time for those in the back: breathe the pricks out.)

You know that guy I was telling you about earlier, who would read my emails and tell management everything? Remember, on average he would piss me off once a week. But he occupied my mind 24/7. I spent literally *thousands of hours* hating him. I would blame him when

I wasn't achieving my goals because I was consumed by the way he made me feel. But I was making myself feel that way. That was *me*! He didn't control my thoughts, I did. I didn't mean it and I didn't want to, but I sub-consciously chose a path that made me feel terrible. I had a choice to be happy or pissed off, and I chose to be pissed off.

I began to speculate about what he had done to me each day behind my back. *He's probably told the boss that I'm not doing enough work. He's probably going to bitch about me when he goes to the kitchen.* Things that hadn't even occurred, but the paranoia and the strength of my prick addiction would invent not just the bullshit scenario but also bullshit evidence to support it. I know it's completely insane, but how many times have we been annoyed at a 'probably' that doesn't exist? All of these 'probablies' added to my baggage of resentment and hatred. My mind was so desperate to hate him that even on the days he didn't do anything wrong, I would make up something to remind myself he was a prick. See how your head will make you suffer not only for things that happened, but for things that haven't actually happened? If we can't nip this in the bud, we're screwed!

I was a fully fledged prick addict. Can you see the similarities between the desperation of drug and prick addicts? I didn't realise, but my old neural pathways needed a prick fix and would do anything to give me one, even if they had to make one up! (All the more reason to burn that pathway down and build another one!) The good news? I've said it before, but I want to reiterate this to you: if your pathway was so strong at creating a life that was programmed for hatred, imagine how strong your pathway could be if you programmed it for self-love, happiness and success. It's pretty exciting.

At the peak of my prick addiction, I felt like I had 1000 kilos weighing down my body. I was receiving everything he said to me as a negative. The look of him made me sick. His eyebrows were like an abandoned house's overgrown lawn – shaggy and uneven. They would move when he spoke. One eyebrow hair was especially long, like even the hair knew that what was beneath it was impossible and it was trying to escape. It would glisten under the overhead lights like an arsehole asteroid plummeting towards Planet Dickface. I'm sure he had gingivitis, because every time he spoke the stench of dead meat would waft into my nostrils. I hated his eyebrows, especially the long eyebrow hair, his breath, the way he clicked the mouse. *(Do you need to click it so hard? Seriously, it's just a little tap, is it so hard to understand? Are you doing it just to piss me off, or is it because I'm pissing you off? You'd better not be pissed off at me. After everything I've put up with, you think you can just sit there and click your mouse like you're King fricking Dick? I hate you!)* If he walked to his office with a coffee, I hated him for not offering to make me one. But if he did offer to make me one, I thought, *Oh, you're just doing this to look good in front of everyone else.*

One day, the boss came in and smiled at me. I felt like screaming at him, *I fuckkkkking haaaaate you for listening to him and making me feel like this. Why are you smiling? What has he told you? What, are you going to fire me because you've believed his lies?* But he really just came into the office and smiled. Meanwhile, Captain Cunt walked over to the photocopier and started hitting buttons and calling the photocopier an arsehole, because he couldn't work out how to scan his time sheet. I looked at him and his one long eyebrow hair. I felt like I couldn't breathe anymore! Was I overdosing on prick? Was there a naloxone shot for this?

I managed to pull myself together enough to whisper, 'I quit you, Captain Prick. I have to see you every day, but I emotionally quit you. You no longer control my thoughts, I'm pulling out of your race, your shit is no longer my shit, you no longer control the way I feel. I QUUUIIIIIT.' I breathed out so deeply, it felt like I was releasing air that had been rotting at the bottom of my lungs. It was like breaking a spell. I started crying at my desk. The emotional weight had been lifted, the guilt I had felt for being such a negative person was gone . . . finally I was free. I would no longer care if he was in a bad mood, I would no longer try to break him out of his moods. He was on his journey and I was on mine.

I went straight into a meeting with management for some promotional ideas, and I thought – while I was on a roll – *I emotionally quit what YOU think of me too. I QUIT YOU!* And by simply trusting myself to be me, I had the best creative meeting of my life, because it freed my mind up to do what I was employed to do.

When we quit pricks, we don't quit ourselves. We still try to succeed, and we still have goals. We just quit the emotional burden of other people and the burden we put on ourselves as a result of those people, which always complicates greatness.

The next morning I walked in and said, 'Good morning, what are you up to?' and this guy looked up at me, rolled his eyes and said, 'It's morning. You ask me this every day and like every other day, nothing is happening.' He rolled his eyes again and went back to his computer. I giggled and responded, 'Righto, want a coffee?' Because he would stay a prick and keep trying to shoot his prick vibes at me. But because I'd quit him, his prick laser could no longer touch me. And you know what? I had a great day at work; the best day I'd had for a very long time. For the first time, instead of letting him control me, I observed his behaviour without any emotion, and he sounded like a negative idiot.

Have you ever had someone dump you and thought you'd never get over it, only to look at that person a few years (or months) later and think, *What was I thinking?*

It felt like that. I found that because I wasn't riddled with anxiety or overthinking, I could give less energy to projects and receive more energy back in results. By emotionally quitting someone, it doesn't mean you give less of a crap about doing things well. It just means that you don't waste your energy on negative people.

This means you make the right emotional investments for you. In my case, my relationships with family and friends improved. My career took off. My soul was buzzing because I had regained my power. And I gave myself permission to follow my own compass.

Now that you've made the emotional decision to quit, you might still have a negative neural pathway spring up and surprise you. You need to burn it down! For so long you have been using this prick as the reason you aren't achieving your goals. But no more excuses. You will feel raw and vulnerable because you no longer have a safety net to justify your reasons for not doing what you want to do. You're the only one controlling you now, and excuses aren't results. Continue to build your positive pathway, continue to strive and be better, continue to ask yourself, *What do I need to do to create this for myself?* Your old pathway would have said, *I can't do this because* . . . But you will have the time and strength to do whatever you want to achieve now. I'm genuinely very excited for you!

Emotionally quitting pricks has changed my life. It took me from being on the brink of unemployment – because if I'd stayed under that prick's power, I would have quit or lost my job – to eventually being part of *The Block*, winning $209,000, buying a block of land, paying off a house, winning a set of lawn bowls in a raffle and starting to play again fourteen years after I retired from the Aussie team (but this time enjoying it), being part of a breakfast radio show in Sydney against my idols Kyle & Jackie O and Amanda Keller, working with a team I adore because we choose to care only about our own shit, selling a TV pilot, being cast on a TV show on 9Life and starting water aerobics. Nobody who knew me expected this turnaround – not even me! But I wholeheartedly attribute it to quitting pricks. I don't do them anymore, though I still have to remind myself of this at times when they sneak into my brain (they're sneaky little buggers!).

Take it from me: if you are a prick addict, you have got to get clean. Don't allow yourself to get your fix, no matter how much your body wants it. Remember, breathe in, breathe out. Keep destroying the old pathway and keep building the new one. Quit the pricks for good!

2

UNMASK YOUR INNER PRICK

*H*ave you ever walked into a room and decided everyone there hates you? I did, all the time! I remember meeting the wives of Norm's mates at a function when Norm and I first started going out. I said hi to them, smiled and pretended I was enjoying myself, but I was already self-programmed to assume they wouldn't like me. The day played out fine with a few wines and some laughs, but there was one girl that would look at me 'weirdly'. In my make-believe, prick-addicted world, I assumed she thought I was a dumb piss wreck and that she didn't like my teeth. I was devastated and hurt that she would think this about me, and vowed never to return to that circle of women again. Even though everything I thought she was thinking about me was being invented by my arsehole of brain: in fact, it was actually what *I* thought of me, not what she thought of me!

My mind did this all the time in the company of other people: my inner (and negative) narrative about myself magically became everyone else's opinion of me. So what's the solution? To be alone all the time so that I'm the only one who will think those things about me? BULLSHIT! Friendships and relationships are the main key to happiness. Sure we can protect ourselves from connecting so we don't have to be confronted with our own demons, but one of those people could be your soulmate or best friend for life. And we shouldn't let our brains rob us of those connections.

Let's look closer at this inner narrative. Maybe every little insecurity has grown your inner prick – the voice in your head that keeps you on the road of destructive behaviour you have created for yourself. Or maybe your inner prick was always inside you but has come bubbling to the surface, like a tsunami of shit, at a particular time for one reason or another.

We weren't born with this narrative of ourselves. At one stage of our lives we didn't have a care in the world except for when we were being fed. No one's born fucked up, we learn how to be. So if we've learnt how to be fucked up, we have the tools within us to learn how not to be fucked up. Identifying our inner pricks plays a huge role in this. Why do we have the voice or the narrative that leads us down the wrong path? Why are we so starved of self-love? If you can't love yourself, you are incapable of loving someone else to your full capacity. You are denying your family, children, partner and friends as well as the true wonderful fantastic you!

Unfortunately, most of us were born into a family with parents who didn't love themselves. It's not their fault; it was a different time. In Australia, self-love has never really been a priority and was often seen as being 'up yourself'. Perhaps you were born because your parents thought they should have children, maybe you were a distraction from their own boring lives or you were a marriage-saving child. The majority of our parents didn't put their souls first, so we are first generation self-lovers and we are working it out for ourselves. It is only now that we are identifying the importance of loving ourselves, as obvious as it sounds.

We grew up emotionally stunted, being told not to brag, show off or make others jealous of our achievements, essentially told not to be proud of our successes. Let's just take a minute to digest how fucked up that is. That someone can be amazing but is told to *tone it down* so they don't make their friends or family jealous. It's a tragedy how much brilliance has been lost in this type of upbringing. Imagine if every child was told to be the best they could, and we had a huge celebration when they achieved something they'd set out to do, no matter how big or small. Wouldn't that be something?

✱

My struggle has been with self-worth. I have a little voice in my head that continues to tell me everyone hates me. I battle with it every day and it never goes away. When I leave a room, my default is to not care about who I've been talking to or developing connections with. Because I assume soon enough they won't like me, and it's just easier to not connect than allow them to know the real me. I cover these thoughts up with a big smile and fake confidence that I use like a costume. But as I work on silencing my inner prick, I am learning how not to be fucked up. How this narrative that holds me back was given to me by other people. It is their shit, not mine.

We grew up in regional Victoria without electricity, powering our house lights with forklift batteries and only able to watch our black and white TV for an hour a night. Which was fine, this was my normal and, really, who cares about electricity if you don't know a life without it? The only bummer with the black and white TV was that kids at school would ask me what colour Power Ranger was my favourite and I would have to respond with 'the grey one'. (There was no grey one.)

My father has always struggled with mental health issues, though they were undiagnosed when I was young. As a kid, I had no idea what was going on; I know he tried his best, always driving me to sporting events and things. What I'm about to tell you is a reflection of the inadequate medical system of the time, and not a reflection of my dad personally.

Because of his undiagnosed mental illness, during my childhood he would fire up with rage and scream, 'I hate you!' to me and my mum. The next day he would be fine, and when I asked why he had said that, he would laugh and say, 'Oh, I was mad last night,' and we would continue life as if nothing had happened.

One day he picked me up from school camp and I asked him to give my friend a lift home as her parents were stuck at work. I knew shit was going down when I saw his eyes had turned into two white marbles, bulging out of his head as he frantically looked left and right. You would always get out of Dad's way when you saw the marble eyes. We dropped my friend at her front door and drove away.

He started screaming, 'I fucking hate you! She's not my kid. Fuck you!'

The car stopped at a stop sign. There was an old 70s red-brick house on the driver's side and a ditch with reeds and grass on my side. I opened the door, ran into the reeds and scrunched down in an upright ball, hiding without a plan. I was fifteen, with no money, and at my age who was going to take my side? I even believed what he was saying about me. My heart was running at a million miles an hour. *What am I doing? I've heard all this before and how am I going to get home?* In my mind, this was my fault because I really shouldn't have asked him to drive my friend home.

He left the motor running and got out of the car, screaming, 'Get in the fucking car.'

Not looking for trouble, I stood up, the reeds reaching my waist, and got back in the car. We didn't talk again during the twenty-minute trip home.

We arrived home and walked through the old flywire door with holes in the netting. As I approached my mother to cuddle her after being away for a week at school camp, my dad said, 'She's been a right royal bitch, so before she fills your head full of any bullshit, I'm just telling you first!'

Each person was living their own journey: Dad was battling, Mum was battling and so was I. Three journeys, three internal narratives, three different potential interpretations of this story.

A few months later I was having trouble concentrating at school. I would get itchy arms when I focused on something for too long, and the thought of looking at a book or assignment was overwhelming. Later in life I would be diagnosed with ADHD, but in this instant we weren't sure if the problem was hormones or me just being a lazy teenager. My concentration would just disappear! When I was playing in the state championship for lawn bowls, I was leading the grand final 20–5, 1 point away from the win. Yet suddenly my concentration left me and I started losing end after end, to finally lose the match 20–21. This inability to focus was having an impact on everything in my life.

My mum took me to the local doctor, who was a family friend, and he asked a personal favour to refer us to a friend of his who was one of the best psychologists in the industry. The appointment would cost $500; Dad was furious and wanted no part in paying for it. So Mum and my grandparents saved up every cent they had until the appointment. We had to drive to Melbourne for it, which was a big deal for us country folk. We packed our lunch and snacks, Grandma paid for the petrol and we set off on our three-hour journey.

I remember sitting in the waiting room and answering questions on a form about whether or not I wanted to harm myself. I now know this is general psychologist stuff, but back then I laughed with Mum as no one ever saw a psychologist in our small town. Mum rubbed me on the arm and said, with a smile on her face, 'You know you aren't mad. This is just to see if there's a reason why you can't concentrate. You aren't a mad bastard.'

When my name was called, we walked down a long white corridor, the walls filled with cheap abstract prints, which were all the rage in the 90s. With butterflies in my stomach, I walked through the door to see a huge mahogany desk with green leather inserts, the walls littered with books from the floor to the ceiling. I peered at a man with a beard sitting behind the desk in a dark brown swivel chair that had buttons running down each side. I'd never seen a chair like that in real life, only in those English movies with royalty that I'd seen on the days I'd walked to Nan and Pop's house to watch TV. I remember feeling like I was in a foreign land. It was a long way from our little electricity-deficient house where Mum had to boil water on the stove to give us kids a warm bath.

The psychologist sat looking at the wall to his side, with his chair swivelled towards a large oil painting of a bunch of flowers.

My mum's voice got shaky, as we were both like Crocodile Dundee when he goes to New York for the first time. 'H-hello . . . nice to meet you and thanks so much for fitting us in.'

He was probably in his sixties, with a short silver beard, an expensive dark-blue suit with a maroon hand-kerchief hanging out of one pocket, and gold and black horseshoe cufflinks. The room smelt like leather and library mixed into one. My mother and I sat on the other side of his desk, around two metres away from him. 'Mmmhmmmmm,' he replied while still facing the side wall, reading my file.

My mother and I sat in silence as he read the multiple choice health questions I'd filled out in the waiting room.

He swivelled his leather chair in our direction, slowly, without making eye contact with us. His eyes darted to the back of the room, then back to the desk where he'd placed my file. He picked it up again and exhaled loudly while flicking through the pages before finally looking up at my mum. 'There's nothing wrong with her,' he said in a stern voice.

Mum let out an awkward 'ohhh', unaware of what was happening as he hadn't asked us anything or consulted with us.

He swivelled his chair back to his original position and returned his gaze to the flower vase oil painting. He let out another big sigh but this time talked to the wall like we were an inconvenience. 'I've looked at her file and there's nothing wrong with her. No need to book a follow-up session.'

My mother looked confused. 'Okay, but we've travelled so far, and I can expla—'

Before Mum could finish the sentence, he cut her off, still looking at his painting, his fingers tapping together in a prayer position. 'And I thank you for coming, goodbye.'

We got up awkwardly. He was still not looking at us and I felt like sinking into the floor. I had wasted this man's valuable time and he was angry at us for that. I had let down our local doctor, who had called in a personal favour to get us the appointment. But most of all, I had wasted Mum and Grandma's money. Grandma had been planning to go on a cruise but gave me her cruise money, while Mum had needed a new pair of shoes but taped the sole of her shoe up with sticky tape to afford this appointment. They had been so proud that they could send me to one of the best, and I was embarrassed that there was nothing wrong with me. I felt like I should have given them their money's worth and been as fucked up as possible so they could justify the expense. Maybe I should have ticked more fucked-up boxes? But Mum had said to tell the truth, and the truth was I did not want to hurt myself. I left that doctor's office embarrassed, guilt ridden and convinced that my inability to concentrate was because I was not trying hard enough. It was my fault! MY FAULT!

Ten years later, when I was 25, I finally worked up the courage to go to another psychologist because I knew something wasn't right. I knew I was different. They diagnosed me with ADHD. We worked on ways to manage it and the tools he gave me have transformed my life.

You see how dangerous your inner prick is? I knew in my gut all those years that something wasn't right, but at the same time the narrative I'd told myself was *not* to trust my gut. It sounded like this: *There's nothing wrong with you. Dismiss this stupid feeling that there is, because if you don't you will be subjected to humiliation and waste everyone's time. You're a fraud, Jess, you're a fraud! You make things up in your head and you fuck it up for everyone!* So on this hugely important issue I took the advice of my inner prick. But think about it: we get second and third opinions for medical procedures, haircuts, even bridal makeup! When it comes to our soul, though, we are willing to jump on any negative bandwagon that will cart away our chance at fulfilment as fast as a runaway taxi. I told myself every day, *I am a bad egg. I am a problem for people. What I feel and my problems aren't real, therefore they aren't important.* But when I got this diagnosis, it was a light-bulb moment: my inner prick was a narrative that I had learnt. It was the words of other people, disguised in my voice, in my head! I had copied and pasted my own interpretation of what people had said to me over the years and created my own story, except, of course, only the negative stuff. Do you think I copied and pasted any of the good stuff? To be honest I can't even remember any. Which is fucking ridiculous. Your brain can not only alter the way you think about yourself in the present, but it can also alter your perception of the past? FUCK YOU, DEEPLY ENGRAINED NEUROLOGICAL HABITS! The narrative created by these neurological pathways was so far from the truth, but the little bastards brainwashed me every day to think this was my reality. And they do it to EVERYONE! Unless you're Tony Robbins. He seems pretty cool with himself.

Along with anger, I also felt forgiveness. And a sense of relief that I wasn't the things I had told myself I was. You should tap into your inner prick and realise that this isn't you either: we've been invaded and held for ransom by a bunch of arsehole-y thoughts for so long. TIME TO FIGHT BACK!

Some of us will have had the same negative narrative since puberty: our pathways of habit have just continued unchanged since then. In a physical sense, we grew boobs and pubic hair, maybe had children, but psychologically we still suffer from the same insecurities. We've gone through physical puberty, but we haven't gone through spiritual puberty. For some of us, it has to be self-induced: stand up for yourself and make changes to find peace and satisfaction where you are right now. You'll do this by controlling the inner narrative of yourself: a new one, a grown-up one, a logical one. Start right now, even if you have to bullshit yourself for a while until you can believe it. You've been bullshitting yourself for ages now anyway by telling yourself you aren't good enough, so why not swing in the opposite direction?

During puberty I wasn't very popular. I played lawn bowls (complete with daggy white clothes), had no electricity so turned up to school smelling like kerosene from the heater, and had the most epic monobrow Australia's ever seen. It's a familiar story: at a time when all you want is to fit in, you're told things like 'you're ugly', 'you're a loser', 'you're a geek'. So of course you pluck your eyebrows so they look like anorexic worms, buy a Chicago Bulls jersey and some hot pants, marinate yourself in Impulse body spray and start kissing the dude in your class most likely to end up in gaol. Because, you know, bad's *cool*. Wag school, get a couple of detentions. The teachers freak out because they think you're going to end up pregnant and drop out of school, so in a desperate attempt to save their former class captain they tell you, 'You are going nowhere with this behaviour. You're acting like a dropkick, and that boy you're hanging out with is a loser.' But the brain only picks up what it wants to, so generally you only hear '**You are going nowhere**' but not '. . . with this behaviour'. And the rest of it? '**You're a dropkick, and** ~~that boy you are hanging out with is~~ **a loser**.' So now you're an ugly, geeky, loser dropkick who's going nowhere. Which then takes on its own lifeform: *You're not worthy, you're terrible at what you do. You're just a waste of space.* I started to hoard evidence which could be used to prove these traits. To the point where, if it went to trial, I would have so much evidence that I was the world's largest cunt even OJ Simpson would look at me in disgust.

Ever had a friend take something the wrong way and become really upset? Chances are you've touched his or her inner narrative. Ever overreacted to an argument with your partner or friend? They've touched your inner narrative. Something that to everyone else sounds so far from the truth, but which is gospel to you. When our inner pricks get provoked it sends us CRAZY. Because it is a deep torture we've been dealing with for most of our life. You aren't crazy! There's nothing wrong with you! You just need to change the habits of thinking about yourself, create a new narrative.

Here's an example for you. Norm jokes with me that I don't do anything around the house (because he genuinely believes I do the majority of the housework and this is his man way of saying 'Thank you'). However, because I'm programmed to think I'm not enough, that I'm not doing a good job at anything, and also because I feel let down because Norm doesn't do as much, I go crazy! It touches one of my core inner narratives and it sends me into a hormonal ball of fucking anger! He then says he was only joking, but that just spirals me into every other narrative about lack of self-worth I have ever felt. I start bringing up that time seven years ago when he went to the strippers and vomited in the shower and I cleaned it up. He looks at me like *Why are you bringing up evidence from years ago about something we'd clearly moved on from?* But that's what the inner narrative does! When someone touches a keyword or feeling from a narrative we've given ourselves, our poor partners cop the brunt of twenty years of anger and pain for a situation that has only happened today.

I wasn't abused or tortured or had one single traumatic event that fucked everything up. And that makes it worse! When you're at home feeling like a pile of ball sacks and you see on the news a woman has been severely beaten for fighting for women's rights, only to then see her smiling with her bandages wrapped around her head vowing to fight another day, you think, *Oh god! What have I got to complain about?* But this is the thing: we all have our own demons. Okay, people might not be trying to murder you (hopefully; if they are maybe put this book down and run!), but your problems are real, too. Don't dismiss them because they feel less valid than someone else's.

Mum split up with Dad when I was seventeen, and he stayed living in the family home for three months until he found a place. He would get me alone and tell me, 'Did you know the reason why your mum left me was because she hates both of us, but she can't kick you out because you are her kid?' He would laugh and say, 'Isn't it unfair that I have to leave because you're a pain in the arse!' I would get angry at my mum and ask her, 'Why would you say that?' She would get upset and tell me it hurt her that I would believe such a thing. We were all locked in our individual prisons of pain. Everyone had their back story, and we each created a narrative from that experience: my dad needed a spiritual release from the rejection of a breakup. My inner narrative was all ears to anything negative.

When Dad moved out, I went with him. He would tell me that we were the same and I was lucky because he would be the only one who ever got me. I felt worthless and hated but because he was repeating everything my inner prick said, I felt like he *was* the only one who got me. In hindsight, it is hard to separate yourself from any person who reinforces your inner prick. To be honest, his inner prick was probably the same as mine, so we just fed each other stories to validate our already thriving negative narratives. Negativity is great company. Oh such great company. There's no greater bond than two people telling each other that everything and everyone in the world hates us except for the two in conversation. It's like a shitty vow of commitment. It's so isolating yet so satisfying. This is because the bad habits you're feeding also validate your own isolation. Every bad habit in your brain is buzzing and at the time it's glorious: a sense of superiority that feeds your ego that everyone on this planet is fucked except for the two of you! Even though, statistically speaking, it's highly unlikely that *everyone* around you is an arsehole.

We lived that way for fourteen months. Then I moved to Melbourne and tried to seek validation and love from anything and anyone I could find. But my inner prick is a terrible judge of character (and I bet yours is too). I ended up drinking a lot and sleeping with anyone who would look at me sideways, just so I could feel one second of affection. I'd walk to Crown Casino to play the pokies, pressing 1-cent spins purely so I could enjoy the lights and sounds. I stopped playing bowls and fell behind in the training drills we were meant to do in our own practice time. I worked in a call centre (the first of many) flogging holiday packages to Hilton members, barely turning up while partying five nights a week. But the emptiness grew within me, fuelled by the one-night stands and low serotonin levels.

Now, before this starts to sound like I've drunk a bottle of the Sad Gin and I'm that chick at the bar telling everyone my 'poor-me tales', stick with me, because everyone involved in this has a happy ending. You know from what I've already told you that I did eventually get my inner prick to shut up for long enough to build a fulfilled life. But before that I had to experience the Christmas Day from hell, when everything my inner prick had ever told me would come crashing down on my head like a ton of bricks.

My dad had left a family trail behind him: four children from an earlier marriage who would come in and out of our lives. They had their own issues, too, not necessarily from him, but from life. I remember seeking their companionship but looking back I can see they had no interest; I was like a desperate boyfriend ringing them all the time and pretty much begging them to be family. But they had their own narratives and their own demons.

I did nearly crack one sister! I couldn't believe it when she called and invited me for a sleepover one Christmas Eve. We went out for dinner and laughed and gossiped all night; it was glorious, just calling someone sis. It was a complete fantasy because we didn't really know each other. It was like when kids play mummies and daddies. This was a game of sisters and sisters, and for a few hours I pretended we had our shit together.

The next morning we cuddled each other for Christmas, I put on a pair of musical reindeer horns to get in the spirit and we exchanged presents. She had a shower, came out in her Christmas dress and said, 'Stay at the house as long as you want! I have to go to lunch with the girls [the other sisters]. Hey, could you do me a favour and not mention to anyone that we hung out? I don't want it to be weird with them.' I felt like when you realise you've been used for a one-night stand. But I also didn't want to cause trouble. I was just happy to have her in my life, so I'd do whatever she wanted not to fuck it up.

Anyway, back to that Christmas Day, I was hanging around my sister's empty house wearing reindeer horns. I jumped on Facebook and remembered my cousins from when I was young – we were Facebook friends but hadn't exchanged messages or anything. When Dad's mum was alive, we all used to hang out as kids. They cut their connection with Dad when Grandma died so I had not seen them since I was twelve. But I remembered being so happy and content at their Christmas celebrations. The tree heavy with decorations, the smell of yummy food, the infectious laugh of one of my aunties, who was so chic because she worked in advertising and had beautiful clothes. It was always so cool at their place in the Christmas heat because they had an air conditioner! That was so flash and fancy for us as kids.

As I looked around my sister's empty lounge room, I thought, *Fuck it, I'm going there! It's Christmas Day, Mum's working, my brother's working. I have nowhere to be or go. It's around 11 am, so if I ring her now, I can be there in time for Christmas lunch. I'll even grab some wine, flowers. I might even sleep the night if they'll have me?* I got that stabbing feeling of excitement in my stomach. Faaaabulous Christmas, here we come! Life's what you make it; you have to make your own luck happen.

I looked through the online White Pages and found the number. I excitedly dialled and it started ringing! 'Please be home, please be home,' I whispered as the phone rang.

'Hellloooooooo?' I heard my aunty answer and someone cackle in the background.

Yessss, I thought to myself, and with a big grin I said, 'Aunty, it's me, Jess.'

'Who?' she asked.

To be fair, we hadn't spoken or seen each other in over six years. 'Me, your niece . . . Jess from Tatura.'

'Oh, Jesssssss,' she said in a surprised high-pitched yet not disappointed voice. 'How are you?'

'Yeah good, I just wanted to say Merry Christmas, and I'm in the area and wondering if I could pop in?'

'Oh Jess, Merry Christmas to you, we would love you to . . .'

I internally screamed with excitement!

'. . . But we are going to my in-laws today. Maybe another time next week?'

Ahhhh, fuck it, but totally understandable. 'Of course. Can you pass on a Merry Christmas to everyone for me?'

'Of course I will, send love to your mum for me,' she replied and we hung up.

Dang it! I wasn't too disappointed because she wanted to see me eventually, so I took that as a win.

I decided to drive three hours home to Mum's house and hopefully catch her at the end of her work shift. But first, for nostalgic reasons, I wanted to see the big gum tree my aunty has in front of her house, which my cousins and I used to play around at Christmas time. I still remembered the address because when I was a kid, Dad used to yell out 'where the fuck is' and the number and name of their street when we were driving there.

As I drove up I saw that the street sign sticks out like dog's balls, so on reflection I don't know why Dad would scream out so much about not being able to find it. I started recognising the houses leading up to their house and the excitement of nearly being there and seeing Grandma and my cousins and presents and icecream! I passed the property with the white fence, then the brick house with the big trees, feeling the same excitement and anticipation as I did when I was six.

I pulled up outside my aunty's house on the corner. Nothing had changed from when I had last seen it six years ago. Actually, what the fuck? *Nothing* had changed, even the cars in the driveway! I saw a woman smiling at the foot of the grease-stained concrete driveway. It was my cousin and she was greeting my uncle who had just arrived. My cousin was laughing and turned her head slightly to the left towards me. Our eyes locked. We stared at each other for about three seconds, which felt like a life-time. Her brunette bob blew gently in the wind and softly over her eyes. I don't know if she knew it was me but she was soon distracted by my uncle asking her to hold some food containers. *They're having Christmas Day at my aunty's house, after she told me they weren't going to be home!*

My heart sank, and the emptiness this time felt worse than a one-night stand. This was some next-level loser alone shit. It was like giving some guy a blow job next to a Salvos donation bin because he said he loved you, and then, as soon as you were done, having him tell you he was only tricking, leaving you next to two bags of clothes and a baby bouncer on the side of the road at one in the morning.

As I sat in my car, numb and feeling stupid, my inner prick reminded me, *Of course they didn't want you around; no one wants to be around you. Get the hint! When people are around you they are embarrassed. How many times does the universe have to show you you're a bad egg! You're a bad person and anything else you're telling yourself is bullshitting!* Notice the narrative? My inner prick was shouting at me from the rooftops.

Feeling like a worthless piece of crap, I was in desperate need of validation. Whenever my inner prick has told me I'm not worthy of something as a person, my general path to seek fulfilment has involved a penis. Yep, the magic penis ride – just like Aladdin and his magic carpet, but instead of holding onto the hem, you hold onto the ball-bag for dear life. Which many of us seek validation from but which generally leaves us feeling emptier than before. If penis was actually a spiritual pathway to validation, they would have huge cocks carved out of stone in Nepal instead of Buddha. They would hand out dildos at church instead of bread and wine. They would have trouser-snake statues for sale at hippie shops that we would take home and light incense around and pray to the almighty cock for good health and happiness for our family. But they don't and that should be a big warning that penis isn't a path to happiness or fulfilment.

So, of course, as I drove away from my aunty's house and my uncle's stupid Tupperware container full of tasty treats and the big gum tree that I now wanted to set on fire, I reached for my phone and called my ex-boyfriend, who lived 3.5 hours away.

We'd broken up twelve months ago and he'd since moved away, but I was hoping he'd be back in town to see his parents for Christmas. For the sake of not getting sued, I'll call him Harry. I'd met Harry at the local footy club when I was a teenager and it was love at first sight when he fingered me on the dance floor. I think you can tell a lot from a fingering; there's a romantic fingering and a one-night-stand fingering, and this one was a romantic 'I'm into you' kind of finger. As 'Mustang Sally' echoed across the footy club rooms, the purple disco light shadowing his pale face and glistening off his almost monobrow, as he looked up at me (he was extremely short), opening his mouth with dried spit at the corners to whisper, 'Chook was wrong about you, you're a sexy bird', it felt like instead of touching my cervix with his stumpy grease-stained fingers, he was really touching my soul.

From that moment on, Harry and I had a whirlwind romance you could only dream of. He would whisk me to the Summernats, which is a race car convention where you watch old utes doing 'skidddddies'. I'll never forget how he smiled at me after a piece of rubber came off a tyre, hurtling its way into the crowd and slicing my face just under my eye. He turned to me, looked me in the bleeding eye and said, 'Better not fucking scar, I hate scars.'

But there were many wonderful layers to Harry; he was like an onion. He knew how to look after his women. He even forgave me once when I drove him home drunk in his 1995 white Holden Commodore. I accidentally hit a kerb and the mudflap snapped off. He told me, 'I should get angry at you because that was a dickhead thing to do, a lot of other people would, but ya lucky I'm a nice guy, so I'll let it go this time.' It was moments like this that made me fall even more in love with him.

I was devastated when he moved to Western Australia to be a tradie. It was a 24-hour drive to see each other but we stayed together. He said he was doing it for us, but I shouldn't bother coming with him because he knew how much I loved my job picking tomatoes. (I told him every day that I hated it, but he said it was an opportunity to really work my way up in the tomato picking industry. Hell, I was illegally being paid $8 an hour! I'd have been mad to give that up.) Him going to Western Australia meant we could both work on our dreams.

Even though he was a tradie, his social media posts showed he had a real passion for tourism. He was being tagged in lots of photos with backpackers, showing them a really good time. I could imagine they were missing their families so he would hug them in the posts. In one photo a poor backpacker must have been feeling cold on her breasts and neck, because beautiful Haz was keeping them warm with his hands and his lips. One little man comforting six Swedish backpackers who were probably missing their brothers and cousins; he was very considerate like that. When I asked him about the photo, he said he was just making sure they received some of that famous Aussie hospitality. He was a very hospitable guy, Harry was. Needless to say, he soon dumped me over text at 1 am on a Sunday and that was the end of that.

Now, on Christmas Day twelve months later, I was calling him in my car as I left Melbourne, desperately seeking validation from the spiritual penis. He was at his home with his family, so I asked if he wanted to meet for 'a lemonade and biscuit', which was our code phrase when we were dating. He told me to call him when I was five minutes away, park one block over, sneak into the back garden shed and he'd meet me there. I finally arrived and redid my makeup, covering the tear streaks with foundation and throwing on some lip gloss. The thought of recapturing what we'd had together gave me another surge of stabbing excitement in my stomach. Maybe this would be the moment he realised we should be together forever. Maybe this time next year I'd be inside that house rather than sneaking into the garden shed.

I tiptoed past the kitchen window where I could hear laughter and beer cans opening, past the hot water service and into the garden shed. I texted him at 4.15 pm: *I'm here,* and again at 4.25 pm: *Are you coming?* I waited another fifteen minutes, perching on a can of paint looking at a fishing rod with dried-up bait on the hook, a rake on my left and a crabbing net to my right. This wasn't even a garden shed, it was a full-of-shit shed. I texted again at 4.40 pm: *Oy I'm here.* Five o'clock was approaching and the 40-degree heat belting down from the summer sun on the tin shed roof felt like it was suffocating me. I heard the sound of something rustling behind me under the milk crates full of power cords. But I wasn't moving! I could not handle another rejection that day. I was going to worship the spiritual trouser snake if it was the last thing I did. But at the same time I didn't want to bother him if he was having a good time with his family, and I didn't want to text him so much that he thought I was a lonely stalker.

Aaaaannnd that was when it hit me. *Jess! You ARE a lonely stalker! You are hiding in a garden shed on Christmas Day! Waiting for a guy who dumped you at 1 am via text, who originally fingered you on a dance floor, who isn't returning your texts . . . while you sit on his dad's can of paint, possibly suffering from dehydration. JUST GO HOME!* I stood up and stretched my back after sitting on that can of paint for over an hour. As I sneaked back past the kitchen window, I could hear Harry talking about a game of footy he kicked the winning goal for three years ago. Somehow I made it out the front gate and into my car.

I felt empty and alone but not surprised. My inner prick had verified this feeling of worthlessness and self-hatred for years. *I'm a bad egg. Shit, I just broke and entered looking for lemonade and biscuits. Jess, get the hint, look at your day. People had to lie about being with you, people had to lie not to see you and people didn't even show up!* What a fucking day for my inner prick to flourish.

But you must understand something: this destructive behaviour isn't the real me, just like your destructive behaviour isn't the real you! This is the detrimental effect of filtering everything you do and say through your inner prick. There was one common train of thought guiding my irrational actions through that horrendous Christmas Day and it was that I was worthless.

But I've told you this story only from my perspective. Let's consider it from the perspective of the others involved for a moment.

My dad wasn't well, and his behaviour alienated him from everyone in his life. He has six children and I'm the only one who still talks to him. He took me to bowls and that was a great stepping stone in my life, so I have chosen to practise gratitude towards him. When you identify the source of your inner prick, you will feel angry and resentful. But the only way to extinguish or rewrite your narrative is to forgive and find peace. Dad has missed out on so many wonderful moments with his family because the demons he battled overtook his life. I spoke to him recently, and he has been studying reincarnation because he's looking forward to dying and being reborn again to start over. We are the lucky ones because we are identifying the source of our demons and we are tackling them. We will have a wonderful life because we are working towards one.

On that Christmas Eve, my sister wanted to see me, but she didn't have the strength to tell 'the pack' that, so she managed the situation as best she could.

My aunty probably thought, *We haven't seen her for so long and we have issues with her dad, so let's start with an intimate gathering. It's Christmas, let's not complicate it.* She didn't know the events leading up to my call or how much I desperately needed to see her.

And Harry? Well . . . you can't wait in a garden shed for penis and expect anything good's going to come of it. He never did text or call back, by the way.

These events wouldn't have hurt so much without my inner prick telling me these things were happening because I'm worthless. Every aspect of my and your life is filtered through our inner prick's narrative. Finding the origin of that narrative? Well, that's the most important step on your journey towards fulfilment.

✷

Let's start the new habits and narratives of ourselves now. Repeat after me: I am fantastic, I am extremely loveable.

If you have a partner: I am lucky to have my partner, my partner is lucky to have me. They have the freedom to do what they like, as do I. Keep going: I take responsibility for the way I feel. It is unfair to blame someone for my lack of peace. I'm starting now. I will fall over, I will stumble, but I am fighting for a life. I am fighting for a life not wasted. I'm fighting for me!

You might be telling yourself, *My life has been fine, uncomplicated up to this point. I have no reference of where this narrative has come from.* NO! You weren't born feeling insecure or with an inner prick inside you. You learnt this narrative from somewhere or someone. Take the time now to ask yourself, when did you first start feeling like this? It doesn't have to be something as significant as hating yourself, but maybe you tell yourself you're fat, or you can't achieve great things because . . . whatever it is, find the moment you first started to tell yourself this story. That is your origin point.

Next, you need to ask, Why did you feel like this? Who started your inner prick growing? Was it school bullies? Was it one (or both) of your parents? Was it a romantic partner? A colleague? Remember, the inner prick speaks someone else's words that you have adopted as your own. So basically, you've been tricked and lied to.

Once you've found the source of your inner prick, you need to make peace with it before you can start changing the narrative. You may never understand how or why it started, and you don't need to be friends with the person (or people) who started it. (You can if you want, but don't rely on someone else's response to your emotional generosity to find peace, because this is about you and only you.) For me, I feel sorry for my dad, as he lost so much quality time and love he could have had with us as a family. But his mental state projected so much hatred, I couldn't imagine what he was feeling on the inside. As he has gotten older, we have spoken about it, but if I were to wait for an apology or for him to realise what it was like to grow up around him, I would never find peace. And that's okay. I don't hate him; I'm not angry at him. I love him because he is my dad and he tried his best. I know people say your best isn't always good enough, and sometimes it isn't. But even the worst people in the world are probably doing their best. It's just that their best is really shit, so we shouldn't let them influence our own lives. We gain nothing by seeking validation from people who have a history of making us feel bad about ourselves.

When you've made peace with the source of your inner prick, it's time to create a new narrative. Please understand that you're worth it, please know that you've been through something unfair that has traumatised you. My inner prick was born when I was around four, so I go back to that moment and look my four-year-old self in the eyes, give myself a big cuddle and try to explain it like I would to one of my own children.

'Hey Jess, you're going to hear some pretty gnarly shit . . .' (sorry, I know there's no swearing in front of a child, but the child is me, so can I swear in front of myself?) '. . . you're going to hear some pretty gnarly stuff about yourself in this lifetime. But I want you to know that you don't have to believe everything you hear. Life is about choices and when your dad says these things to you, please know he isn't well. You also live in a time when mental illness isn't recognised. So I know it's a bit of an ask, but could you just not take any notice? These are just words and not life lessons.'

Now it's your turn. Go to yourself as a child, just before your inner prick began spouting rubbish about you. Give that child a huge hug, look into their eyes (your own eyes) and tell them it's going to be okay. Promise that child you won't let the inner prick rule you for the rest of your life. If you can't promise to love your present self, promise to love the innocent and cute child you're looking at. Because every child deserves the best chance at happiness and fulfilment. By lowering the inner prick's volume, you'll finally be able to hear the voice of the real you. The one that has dreams and goals and feels self-worth and love.

✘

So you're feeling good because you've identified the source of your inner prick, made peace with it and started telling yourself a new story. But there's one final thing your inner prick will do to mess with you, and that is to make you a negative narcissist. We usually associate narcissists (or anyone who thinks the world revolves around them) with egomaniacs who care only about themselves in a positive sense. But it can also be narcissistic to presume that we have directly influenced someone's negative mood. Those of us with low self-worth or anxiety might see a colleague/boss/friend/partner in a bad mood, and the first assumption that pops into our head is *What have I done?* or *Are they angry at me?* Because we sit at the centre of our own universe, it's a natural reaction to see someone with the horrendous shits and assume responsibility. Of course, if you've actually done something awful to someone that you know has affected them, the question of 'Are you angry with me?' is null and void, because you KNOW they are. But what I'm describing as negative narcissistic behaviour is when you assume someone's bad day is your fault without any evidence. And we all bloody do it! It doesn't mean you are a horrible person. It just means you have developed a negative narcissistic habit.

Negative narcissism comes from our inner prick exaggerating our insecurities. Generally, those who feel negative narcissism are not self-entitled or selfish. Yet if you look at it in the context of thoughts opposed to emotions, it twists some of the least entitled people into thinking that someone else's headspace is dominated by them. It's absurd!

To work out if you're falling into the negative narcissist trap, ask yourself, is everything around you a direct attack on you? In all honesty it's probably not, so if you answered yes, check what filter you are running this through.

To break this habit, you need to remind yourself that you are not the centre of everyone else's universe. I have to remind myself of this all the time! At the radio station, I walk past the boss on my way to the toilet in the mornings. If I don't get a huge grin from him and a greeting like he is playing the lead in *The Sound of Music*, I assume I've had a really bad radio show, he's already looking for my replacement and I will need to apply for a work-from-home telemarketing job on Seek to pay the bills. I go to the disabled toilets, look at myself in the mirror, prepare myself for the worst, do a nervous poo and get up the courage to walk past him again. As I do, I watch his face like a pervy stalker looking through a bathroom window at shower time. I try to read the mood of his arm and body movements, searching for any evidence that I'm fired. When he looks up from his computer, gives me a huge grin and says, 'Great show today,' I breathe a sigh of relief and cancel my imaginary cover letter for the door-to-door light bulb salesperson job. Of course, once I actually talk to him, I find out he's hurt his back over the weekend and is in pain. (Oh, what? This guy has other stuff going on in his life, and I do not cause every one of his physical and emotional reactions? How odd!) If a man cannot have a sore back and smile weakly at his employee without that employee thinking she is being fired, that is a clear sign of negative narcissism.

You aren't the centre of anyone's universe but your own, so assuming that you are the reason for other people's problems, without any evidence, is a bit negatively up yourself. And if you're going to be up yourself, at least enjoy it and assume, without any evidence, that everyone thinks you're hot. That's a much better way to enjoy your narcissistic tendencies!

Sometimes people just get the shits, the end! Do you need them to like you right now? So badly that, rather than allowing a frustrated person the space to blow off some steam, you would prefer to interrupt them so you can feel loved again? This feeling is about you and not them. So leave them alone and go have a wine with someone who wants to hang out with you. This will feed your soul and allow you to draw strength from a good situation rather than wallowing in a bad one.

Your inner prick has created a skewed narrative of who you think you are. YOU ARE NOT THESE THINGS! You are twisting everything narcissistically to validate your inner prick. I've been there, and I understand, it's so believable. But it's also ruining your life. It's robbing you of your authentic self as you change your behaviour and personality to make people like you. Your authentic self will be received and loved so much more than the character you are trying to represent. The world deserves to know the unapologetically fabulous you . . . not the trying-to-impress-friends you, not the trying-to-fit-in you, not the trying-to-be-a-model-parent you. THE REAL YOU! And once you show people your authentic self, you'll put them at ease to be their authentic selves as well.

More importantly, being a negative narcissist around the wrong people is like handing someone a gun and asking them to shoot you in the self-confidence. If you assume everything is about you, but in a negative fashion, some people who are easily persuaded will start thinking this too. Say you're in a relationship and you accept responsibility for your partner's mood, even though your partner (or other negative narcissist target) might tell you it's not your fault. This will give you a quick ego buzz that you might yearn for, and you might start accepting responsibility for more things, just to get that feeling. However, humans are creatures of persuasion and habit. You are handing a scapegoat to the people around you as a reason for their problems, so they will start to blame you when things go wrong. The destructive cycle will continue, your self-worth and confidence rotting away. You are branded as that person now; you have not stood up for yourself in years. You start to think these people are unfair and egotistical. Part of this is true, but you also need to take the blame. You have voluntarily assumed ownership of all the negative behaviour around you. STOP IT!

You must create new habits with the people around you now. They will be shocked at first to hear you stand up for yourself. But just as you have branded yourself a negative narcissist, you can rebrand yourself a positive legend. It's freaking hard, I know. Sometimes agreeing for the sake of avoiding an argument is the best option. But not ALL the time. You're currently at war with yourself and you need the good to win!

Stop living up to the expectations of your inner prick. Write down five positive dot points about how your authentic self would like to live. Here are my five:

1. I want to be emotionally available for my friends and family.

2. I want to live spontaneously.

3. I feel happiest when I am camping; I want to do more of that with my family.

4. I want to see good in people around me.

5. I want to live a life free of complications.

What are yours? These five dot points are now your commandments. That's your new expectation of the way you're going to live your life. The narrative of *I'm a bad mum* or *I'm a failure because of*... doesn't exist. The five dot points do, though. Read them out loud every day until you have them firmly in the driver's seat for your thoughts and actions (turf that inner prick out of the car at the next traffic lights). Whenever you relapse and start accepting responsibility for other people's problems, and you WILL, go back and sit with your five dot points.

✶

By identifying your inner prick, quitting it and realising when you're being negatively narcissistic, you will cleanse your soul so you can start increasing your self-worth and confidence, which will give you a strong foundation to build your authentic self. Normally, people say the world deserves to see you shine, but I say fuck the world: YOU deserve to see and feel your own shine.

DIVE DEEPLY INTO SELF-BELIEF

*T*here's one common factor that continues to hold us back from our goals and finding our true meaning in life. It's a lack of belief!

When we hear about belief, we usually think about having the power to achieve anything, the belief we can make a million dollars or *insert every other self-belief novelty book or podcast you've read or listened to here*. People say to you, 'Ohhhhh, just believe in yourself' and you think to yourself, *No worries, dickface, I'll just do that and all of my worries will disappear.*

But the term self-belief has a much deeper meaning. What is the intent behind your belief? What is it that you're actually believing in? Is it yourself or your task or both?

This deeper self-belief is built around the core beliefs that you are deserving and worthy of your desires. If you work on cementing these beliefs first, then the belief that you can achieve anything will not only come naturally, it will also be associated with everything in your life, not just the task at hand. This internal process will give you fulfilment and success on many different levels.

Achievements and success via nailing a spreadsheet or being promoted won't fulfil you. Don't get me wrong, these feel good at the time but that sense of pride will dwindle. Your belief needs to come from within. If you don't believe that you deserve and are worthy of any success that comes your way, it will feel like a lucky break or a fluke.

Imagine if you changed your mindset from, 'Oh, I'm so lucky that person gave me a job,' to, 'I deserved that job and I'm going to do so well at it; I aim to be promoted in six months.' It might not necessarily happen, but the thought process will naturally make you strive to be better in your current situation. Because guess what, you aren't lucky (unless you've won a yourtown prize home), you have deserved everything you've achieved in this lifetime! No one achieves anything through luck. Have a read of chapter 7, 'Find your worth at work', to confirm this.

What breaks my heart is seeing people not believe in themselves enough to enjoy their successes or wins. On the outside you might be celebrating, but if you are telling yourself that you didn't deserve it, your mind will succumb to that narrative. There's no point being confident on the outside if you are really thinking the opposite. It's like having a Ferrari with no motor. It looks great in pictures, it makes others think you're doing well, but you can never really go anywhere.

I had a girlfriend who got her dream job. But instead of going into her new workplace confident and excited, she was riddled with the anxiety of not wanting to 'stuff it up'. In her first month, she met her targets and the boss came in to congratulate her. While telling me the story, she said that she didn't believe his praise and thought he was just being kind to motivate her, because she felt she wasn't doing a good job. Naturally she wasn't enjoying herself, because she had no BELIEF she was worthy of the job, despite gaining the job, meeting her targets and getting praise from the boss.

It's a lack of self-belief that robs us of these moments. I want you to give your negativity a face from one of those line-up photos you see on the crime shows. Your self-belief robber has scabs on their cheeks from too many drugs and a huge scar down their forehead from a knife fight when they were trying to steal someone else's self-belief and the victim fought back. Your lack of self-belief is a criminal because they are stealing every piece of your self-worth. You wouldn't leave your front door open for someone to rob your house, but you constantly leave your emotional door open to allow someone to rob your self-belief.

You need to actively battle this robber. Every second they are robbing you of fulfilment or happiness is a second too many. Emotionally taser the bastard! Coathanger them! Every time they tell you that you fluked something, reply, 'No, I didn't. I deserved it because of these reasons . . .' If you can't think of any, ask yourself why others would say you deserved it and use their reasons as your own. You're training your mind to love yourself, so just keep saying it until you start to mute old scarface!

✻

We have been told to associate self-belief with results. That's not true! It's the story we tell ourselves when we achieve those results.

When I was a state champion lawn bowler, I would be training or playing tournaments at Tatura Bowls Club every weekend. It was in the 90s so I had to wear long white pants, white shoes, a white blouse that had the old-school design of a frilly collar, and a wide-brimmed white hat. (On a side note, one day when I was bowling I got my period for the first time . . . in white pants!)

Imagine a freckly-faced fourteen-year-old in old ladies' clothing and that was me, just rolling bowls up and down the green for seven hours a day. The bowls club was next to the public pool, separated by a rickety old six-foot aluminium fence with poles that were ten centimetres apart, so the bowling green was in easy view. Every weekend at least ten kids from my school would gather by the fence to tease me. They would go off to jump in and out of the pool, but they always returned to their front row seats back at the pool fence, icecreams in hand, to continue their favourite weekend activity of mocking me. They would yell out, 'Jess is a siiiiign', because a sign swings back and forward like a bowler's arm. 'Jess is a siiiiign . . . swinging back and forward. Jess is a siiiiign . . . swinging back and forward.'

One day I remember looking up at my grandmother, who was bowling with me. She had her red lipstick on that matched her glasses, the smell of her lavender perfume consuming my nostrils like she was trying to exterminate my social life.

I had tears in my eyes as I said, 'Ma, I don't want to do this. They are making fun of me. I feel stupid.'

She asked, 'Do you dislike playing or do you dislike those kids making fun of you?'

'I don't like the kids making fun of me.'

'You'll thank me later, but never make a decision in life based on the way people make you feel. Those that mock are weak. You remember that when you see someone having a go at something.'

Unaware of what she meant, I looked at her brushing a fly away from my face, tears still leaking from my eyes as I tried to hold them in. 'Does this mean I can't quit?' I asked with a shaky voice.

'You can do whatever you want,' she cackled, and I could see red lipstick smeared on her front two dentures. 'But you have Nationals next week. Do you want to play?'

'Yes, of course.'

'Then don't run away from what you love because you're worried about someone else's reaction, because you will feel ten times worse when you don't do what makes you happy because you're trying to impress someone else. It might make you feel good for a minute, but it won't make you feel good for long. It's a false economy . . . anyway, they're fuckers.'

I choked on my own saliva because Grandma never swore and chuckled back to my bowls. I heard the mocking again and it still hurt but I tried not to listen. Three weeks later I became national champion, my grandmother by my side.

So this sounds like a really positive and inspirational story, right? If I was on an inspirational speaking tour, I'd end the conversation there, drink my wine, sign my books and leave you with the clear message that you don't listen to people putting you down. No shit, Sherlock, great advice! Okay, I'll just turn off the haters like a light switch and my life will be glorious.

But this is where inspirational stories suck. Because you don't just have a change of mindset and then live happily ever after. We are talking about the human mind here; it tries to screw with us. But successful people don't usually mention this, so when we have negative thoughts we just assume we weren't born with an elite mind and we must settle for less. NO! There's no such thing as an elite mind. These people have just surrounded themselves with people who teach them to believe they deserve and are worthy of their success.

These beliefs are critical, because I didn't believe I deserved my success. I didn't believe I was good enough and decided I'd achieved the national trophy because I got lucky. I was ashamed of the trophy, and when people told me I'd played well, I would look at the ground and say, 'Thanks, looks like I fluked it.'

For some reason it is engrained in the Australian culture that if you are proud of your achievements, you're a show-off. But if you look at people who are truly fulfilled, they aren't screaming, 'Look how good I am.' They simply have a confidence about them. I met the Dalai Lama years ago at a conference. During question time I said to him, 'Thank you for your teachings. You have helped me and my family, so I can't thank you enough.' He replied, 'You're welcome,' with a smile on his face. So if the Dalai Lama can accept a compliment, I'm sure you can manage it without worrying about looking cocky or up yourself. Even if you practise it first without truly believing it. Just start the narrative to get the ball rolling, and this will begin the process of gaining self-belief.

A few years after I won the national championship, I was called up to play for my country. I felt bad because I knew a girl called Amy really wanted to play, and I felt like I had taken the position away from her. I felt she deserved it more than I did, despite the fact that I was the obvious choice as an Australian and state champion. On the day of the match, we walked out to a crowd of 50–100 people sitting around and clapping. Everyone asked me if I was excited. In my green and gold cap, I looked at them and gave my standard answer of, 'Oh yes, I am thrilled to be playing for my country. It's always been a dream.' Which it had! So why did I feel empty and alone instead of having the greatest day of my life?

BECAUSE I DIDN'T BELIEVE I DESERVED IT! I DIDN'T BELIEVE I WAS WORTH IT! I thought achieving my goal would make me believe in myself. But it turns out I needed to believe in myself to enjoy my achievements.

My self-worth was so low, I assumed the crowd was there to see everyone else. I assumed the selectors had thrown me a bone and the others were better than me. My lack of self-belief robbed me of that moment!

As the tournament went on I won my games, all of them . . . easily. But instead of celebrating each win and getting a massive rush of joy, I would shake my opponent's hand and say, 'I'm so sorry.' What the fucking fuckity fuck, Jess? I felt as if I'd robbed the opponent of their victory . . . which I had. It's called winning!

Please remember this when something good happens to you. Don't apologise for achieving something great. You deserve every success in the world and part of that journey is the buzz of enjoying it. The saying goes, 'Never let anyone take that away from you,' but really the only one who can take that away is yourself. A lack of self-belief is robbing us of little wins every day.

A millionaire entrepreneur called Dean Graziosi tells a story about a grandmother telling her grandson about two wolves inside your head, a good wolf and a bad wolf, and they're constantly involved in an internal struggle. The bad wolf tells you that you aren't good enough, you aren't worthy and not to believe in yourself. It robs you of confidence, leaves you like an empty shell and dominates your mind. The good wolf reminds you to love yourself, take care of yourself and focus on being the best person you can be.

The little boy asks his grandmother: 'Which wolf wins?'

The grandmother replies with, 'Whichever wolf gets fed the most.'

Regain and celebrate your identity as the wonderful tiger or tigress that you are. Don't let anyone or anything steal your roar ever again!

✗

Let's try an exercise to help this all sink in. I want you to visualise a plank of wood on the ground around 30 centimetres wide and three metres long. Can you walk along that plank? YES, easily, with your eyes closed. Now visualise the exact same plank, but it's fourteen metres up in the air. Below you is a pond full of broken glass, crocodiles, poisonous sea snakes and three hungry great white sharks. It is almost certain death if you fall off the plank and into this pond. Can you walk the plank now? Chances are you'll be a little more hesitant with your answer.

Why? What I asked you was the exact same task, just under different conditions. Your self-belief was high when the plank of wood was on the floor, because there were no negative thoughts to distract you. But your self-doubt affected your self-belief with the second option, because you focused on what could happen if you fell from the plank. It's exactly the same task, but you used your energy to tell your belief system that you were not capable of it.

Since you know you can easily walk that plank when it's on the ground, shift your focus to the task and not what can go wrong. Every time you find yourself thinking, *What can go wrong?* change the question to, *But what can go right?* This is your belief fuel and it's the expensive premium stuff, so your mindset will run like a Ferrari after practising this for just a few weeks. You're reading this book, so you have already shown yourself you want and deserve better. You wouldn't have invested this much time if you didn't, so be assured it's there. Don't allow the negativity of the world and your bad wolf to drown your excellence ever again.

It can be a big shift, though, and sometimes you just want to sit down and cry and think, *Where do I start?*

I read these sorts of self-help books when my son was two months old and I was on maternity leave but, to be honest, I struggled finding the time to even brush my hair in the morning, let alone change my entire psyche to enjoy my successes. You may as well have asked me to build the freaking Eiffel Tower with a toothpick! The idea of achieving fulfilment, combined with the guilt you feel about putting your happiness before others', can be so overwhelming and unattainable you don't even bother. Yet the ripple effect of mentally giving up on yourself is bad for the whole family. Much better to have a powerful, happy, strong mother or sister or friend! You can start believing in yourself with baby steps, through tiny break-throughs, doing something you never felt you were worth or had the time for. LIKE BRUSHING YOUR HAIR! *Start small, Jess, start small,* I said to myself, one step after another. And I learnt that what I thought was impossible last week was totally doable, and the only thing stopping me from me doing it was the narrative I told myself. For goodness' sake, I pushed a human out of my vagina. If I could do that, then I could start brushing my hair!

With each small step, you'll realise you are capable of far more than you ever imagined. The hair-brushing was a small thing, but for me it was a breakthrough and a wake-up call that I was being screwed by my inner narrative. It was really starting to give me the shits. You're worth it! I'm worth it. We are all worth it!

Think back to a time when you won something or did well. It might be from your school days. Perhaps you won a race at school sports, achieved a good grade or won an art competition. Visualise what happened, who was there. You might have been young, but do you remember what that felt like? Feels good, doesn't it? Don't dismiss this feeling as something from the distant past. You have every tool to keep winning or achieving. The only difference between that day and now is that you were part of the race back then. If we liken it to fishing, you had a line in the ocean. You didn't always get a bite but you were in the game. So let's start fishing and get you actively involved in the game again.

If I was in front of you right now, I would be looking you straight in the eyes and saying, 'YOU DESERVE IT!' I'm begging you to listen to me. You have a soul, a mind, a life, so please ignite that flame now. You know why? Because you have one shot at this journey of life and there's no solid evidence of what happens when we cark it.

Imagine you're at an all-you-can-eat buffet. You try to get your money's worth, right? You think, *Okay, I'm going to try everything!* You gorge yourself so full, you feel like you're going to be sick. But fuck it, you've paid your money and you're going to get the most out of it. You encourage the people on your table to go one more plate. If you saw someone you knew at an all-you-can-eat buffet and they had an empty plate, it would be confusing. What if that person said to you, 'Oh, I know I'm at the buffet, but I don't think I deserve to eat. I think I might just sit back and watch everyone else eat and enjoy it. I really can't be bothered going to the bain-marie.' It would be perplexing! But YOU are at the all-you-can-eat buffet of life. You have so much to taste and sample.

Sometimes people in your life might tell you that you're not capable of doing something. But let's run this through the all-you-can-eat buffet scenario. Just as you are lifting the ladle to serve yourself some butter chicken, a fellow diner might say, 'Oh, you can't eat chicken; why bother trying?' Or before you even get up from the table, they might say, 'I know you want to sample the spaghetti bolognaise, but you have never tried it. So why don't you just stay at the table and eat some bread? You know bread, you've done bread before.' First of all, you would think that person is a dickhead. Secondly, you would probably eat as much spaghetti bolognaise as you could out of spite.

The belief in yourself is one of the hardest things to nail within your own psyche. When we doubt ourselves, we feel alone, and then we marinate in our isolation of not feeling worthy. But guess what? Everyone feels it. And even though we talk about fuelling the belief in ourselves, doubt will always creep back. We just try to find techniques that will banish it when it does.

As I've said, even the most successful people in the world suffer from doubt, so you aren't the first person to think you aren't good enough. Did you know that when Hugh Jackman first started playing Wolverine he struggled and was really nervous. Hugh Jackman was nervous! Then he found out he might be sacked from his illustrious Hollywood gig before it finished filming. Angry, he went home to tell his wife, Deb, complaining at 'an Olympic level'. Deb gave him some excellent advice: she told him to stop worrying so much. She told him to trust his instincts, and himself. Thankfully, he listened to her and did just that. And he went on to play Wolverine for thirteen more years.

When we hear a voice, any voice, telling us that we aren't good enough, giving up on our dreams can be an easy exit plan. We assume the people who are telling us are experts in 'us', but only we know what we are capable of. And this is where doubt can actually be your secret fuel. When doubts creep in – self-doubt or external – you have two options. One: to fight. Fight and prove them wrong. Rely on your authentic fantastic self and rise above and win. Or two: play into the expectations of the non-experts and their shitty narrative. Which will you choose? Which one did freaking Wolverine choose? Could you imagine if Hugh Jackman gave in to the doubt?

The thought of Hugh Jackman not being full of himself blows my mind. But I suspect that he and many other successful people use their self-doubt as a rocket engine to take them to the next level: to make them try harder, fight harder. And sure, I also know people who don't suffer from self-doubt and just think they're amazing. I'm sure you can think of a few people like this. But non-doubters, although happy, might actually be held back by their ignorant confidence, because in their minds they can't get any better. Of course, we all just want to be happy, and it takes all sorts of people to make up this earth. But if you ARE a self-doubter, you have been gifted the greatest superpower to perform and to have a very positive life.

Even the legendary Michael Jordan doesn't see himself as a legend. He famously said, 'I have missed over 9000 shots, lost almost 300 games, on 26 occasions I was trusted with making a game-winning shot and I missed it. I have failed time after time in my life and that is why I have succeeded.'

The thing that made Michael Jordan and so many others great is they never let their self-doubt get the best of them. Whether you want to achieve a business goal, master a new hobby, chase your passion or just find some plain old fulfilment, you've actually got this; you just need to believe it.

You know what every single person who has achieved their dream has in common? They started chasing it. And so should you! The great thing about starting is there is no deadline. So you can start right now. Write down what your perfect year would look like. Imagine yourself in twelve months reflecting on this perfect year. What does it say?

Once you've written it, read over it again. Now I want you to change the way you perceive that document. That's now your list of goals, not a creative story. You've just told yourself exactly what you want to do with the next twelve months of your life. You gave yourself permission to write from your soul, because it wasn't real. It gave you the freedom to write without worry or fear of failure. If you didn't write it out, think of your perfect year and apply the same technique.

Now without wanting to sound like a Nike ad, just do it. Start the process of belief! This is me in a holey pair of Norm's undies and an old maternity bra firing the starter gun. Your time starts now.

Belief conquers all, and the difference between excellence and average is a person's willingness to give up on their belief.

Stephen King's famous first book was *Carrie*. But after writing the first few pages, he 'crumpled them up in disgust and threw them away', because he didn't want to waste his time on a story he thought wouldn't sell. The next night, he came home to find his wife, Tabitha, holding the pages. She'd seen them in the bin, read them and wanted to know what happened next. Tabby convinced Stephen to keep going with the draft, the book was later published and has now sold over 350 million copies. But just like you and me, he had a weak moment of self-doubt. He was ready to give up, right at the start of his *Carrie* journey. It was the belief of his wife that helped him go on. But it was also the belief within himself that made him listen to her. Please remember this when your friends are telling you what's great about you. It takes just as much belief to listen to someone giving you compliments and believe them as it does to tell yourself.

Elvis was knocked back after auditioning as a singer for a band and told to stick to driving trucks, which was his day job at the time. Because we know he succeeded, it sounds like an inspiring story of how strong-willed he was, but at the time he must have been freaking the fuck out! I have no doubt Elvis would have drunk a bottle of whiskey and smoked a packet of ciggies in his holey jocks, hand in head and thought, *Shit. What am I doing with my life; am I just chasing a dream?* But his inner belief system must have kicked in for him to think, *I'll try again and see how I go.*

Marilyn Monroe, while trying to be a model and actress, was told to be a secretary instead. If Marilyn was given this advice today, do you think she'd say okay, jump onto Seek with a bottle of sav blanc and filter her job search to 'admin'? No way. She wanted more, like you do, so she kept going.

And, seriously, who has the right to tell you what you're capable of? Only one person in this universe does – it's you!

Once again, there is very little difference between someone chasing their dream and someone who has achieved it. They both want the same thing. The only difference is society tends to judge those still chasing their dream: 'They'll never make it. I don't know why they're trying.' But this was said to Marilyn Monroe! These days, the people who said it to Marilyn would look like fuckwits. But if she had listened to them and become a secretary, those people would have looked like they had the power.

Moral of the story: people who judge you for chasing your dreams are pricks. When you encounter them, go back and read chapter 1 again, so you can emotionally quit them.

But we also need to work on your self-belief so those cunts don't affect the way you live your life.

✱

Sometimes your self-belief robber uses other people as unwitting accomplices. We interpret other people's words in line with what we believe about ourselves. Imagine a professional basketball player has just played a blinder of a game. The coach comes up to him afterwards and says: 'Great game today. You killed it. Just be careful of those three-pointers; they're tough to get on this court.' Now let's see what two different types of mindsets would hear from that conversation.

Mindset full of self-belief: *I killed it and I am on track to be a champion. I'm so thankful the coach told me about those three-pointers. If they think I'm good now, watch how good I'll be when I perfect those!*

Mindset without self-belief: *Are you fucking joking me? I play a good game and I get told to work on my three-pointers? This guy is an arsehole. He's so negative. He's out to get me!*

Because the player with this mindset doesn't believe in himself, he only hears what he isn't good at. He's completely ignored that the coach also told him what a great game he played. He's completely ignored his own observations of playing well. He needs the validation of his coach, because he can't find the validation within himself. The only words that player wants to hear are, 'You're a champion,' and even then without the internal validation or belief, he'll never be truly happy or fulfilled. He won't improve and become a champion, because his own lack of belief won't allow him to work on his faults. His lack of achievement will continue to feed his lack of self-belief.

It becomes a vicious cycle, so working on this area of your life is like preparing the soil to plant the seed.

How many times have you been upset over something someone said to you, but when you raise it with them, they remember saying something completely different? You might put it down to them lying or causing trouble. But could it be that you absorbed the conversation in accordance with your own self-belief? We generally don't remember the exact words of a conversation, but we sure remember the way a conversation makes us feel. If we lack self-belief on a certain subject that comes up, we will go into primal survival mode. We will feel the emotion, digest a few words from the conversation and re-create it in our minds to align with our insecurities. Instead of that person saying something awful, it was probably your self-belief robber striking again! You know the saying 'We touched a sore point'? If someone was to touch you softly, it wouldn't normally hurt. But if they touch you softly on an open wound (in this case, your lack of self-belief), the pain can be intense!

This is another example of how deeply important self-belief is. Having someone touch on your lack of self-belief can make you fly off the handle like a bucking bull. People will think you are irrational, so when you have a real problem, they'll dismiss you as overreacting again.

Go ahead and subconsciously throat punch that robber. And I don't want to get too gender specific, but if your robber's a guy, subconsciously punch him in the scrotum. (This is just an example, of course. I love men, probably too much, to be honest, so this isn't a subconscious dig. Maybe your robber is a turtle? If that's the case, subconsciously taser the shit out of its shell.) This is YOUR time! Stop being a victim of emotional crime.

If you went through the Macca's drive thru, and as the guy serving you was passing you the chips, he said, 'Oh by the way, I'm a dentist and I see you might have a wisdom tooth coming through. Would you like me to jump in your car and take a look at your molars?' You'd think, *Get away from me, you perverted freak! You're dangerously unqualified to do that. I don't believe you're a dentist and wanting to professionally observe the inside of my mouth. I'm reporting you to your manager!*

Are you driving away from that drive thru worried about your wisdom teeth, or feeling bad because you didn't let the pervert look in your mouth? NO! Because he's not a dentist and didn't mean well. So why would you give the power to someone who is also under-qualified to tell you not to believe in yourself or allow you to strip your self-belief away?

DON'T DO IT. Focus instead on feeding the good wolf and stopping the self-belief robber. Write down your perfect year as if you've just lived it and use that as your script for the next twelve months to achieve what you want. Oh, and have a glass of wine, if you drink.

Remember that achieving success isn't a result of luck, so never discount your wins ever again, no matter how big or small!

4

DON'T BOARD
THE ARSEHOLE
TRAIN

Toot toot, you're a passenger on the arsehole train. Can I get you anything to eat? Maybe a shit sandwich? Can I please check your wanker tickets to make sure they're validated? Oh yes, thank you sir/madam, they're right in date, you're actively using the arsehole train, and you're recruiting new passengers you've never even met.

The arsehole train is a bit like the ripple effect in water. Someone takes their bad mood out on you, which puts you in a bad mood, which you pass onto someone else, who gives it to someone you might not even know.

Let me give you an extreme example that happened to a girl I used to work with. She'd once had a boss who went through a messy divorce; one day his ex-wife had come to his house and spray-painted 'arsehole' on his car, because he didn't want to part with any of his super. Don't know if this was fair, don't care; it's not our problem and not our shit to take on. But he turned up in a FOUL mood that day, and nobody knew why at that point. All my girlfriend knew was that the crow's feet on the side of his eyes looked like valleys of anger as he squinted his face in a condescending way to anyone who spoke to him.

Remember in chapter 2 when I talked about negative narcissism, where we think everything's our fault, because we are each the centre of our own universe (but not the centre of the actual universe)? Well, my girlfriend was being a negative narcissist and she took her boss's bad mood rather personally. She had been working hard and couldn't think of a reason why he would be acting so childish and mean to everyone, especially her. She didn't deserve this, how dare he not sing hello and the praises of everyone in the office. This then put her in a foul mood (*toot toot*, another passenger boards the arsehole train), which started touching on her own insecurities like being undervalued, mistreated, taken advantage of etc. She left work, taking her foul mood home.

Her husband, a plasterer, came home after a long, physically exhausting day. He kicked his shoes off at the door and some plaster fell onto the tiles.

My girlfriend snapped, 'What the fuck? I clean this house. I am sick of being undervalued and mistreated!'

Her husband, who had been expecting a 'Good evening, honey, how was your day?' was shocked at this reception and unaware of the events leading up to it. (*Toot toot*, another passenger on the arsehole train!) He responded with, 'Well get fucked then!' He put his shoes back on and drove angrily to his local pub to have a beer with the boys and talk about how his missus must be hormonal.

On the way to the pub, a car pulls out sharply in front of him. My girlfriend's husband, still fuming, beeps aggressively. The guy who'd pulled out in front of him, who I suspect had boarded an arsehole train on a different line, jumped out of the car. Husband jumped out of the car as well, because he'd had enough of being yelled at that night and was taking that emotional suitcase with him on his arsehole train journey.

They got into an argument that turned physical. Husband got punched in the right side of his temple, smashing him to the ground where the bitumen hit the other side of his head. Husband was unconscious, blood seeping from his right ear and slumped on the side of the road. Obviously the guy who'd hit him was freaking out so he called the ambulance.

When my girlfriend was called, she felt terrible and rushed to the hospital (notice when a real problem arises, it makes the small problem that had consumed your world seem like nothing?). The news was not good when she arrived. Her husband had suffered severe brain damage. He would live but he would not walk again; he would not talk properly again; the man she'd married would never be the same again.

The man charged with his assault claimed he had been fighting with his new partner. She was going through a divorce and had just found out that after not working and raising her children with her ex-husband for almost twenty years, her ex was challenging the super split, effectively leaving her broke in her old age. The stress of this caused problems with her new relationship as, *toot toot*, she was on her arsehole train and wary of trusting a man again because she felt tricked by her ex-husband. Who, you've probably guessed, was my girlfriend's boss. *TOOT FUCKING TOOT!* Get me a tequila shot to carriage five, please . . . mind blown!

This is a perfect example of the ripple effect of someone taking their mood out on others. When you see someone on the arsehole train, you can choose whether to board it or not. Yet you have to understand that by boarding it, you will recruit extra passengers, and do you really want to do that?

There are so many different people boarding so many different arsehole trains. The trains circle around each other, picking up more people on the way. The six degrees of separation is phenomenal in that a complete stranger could be rude to you, and there's a chance that, three years ago, you might have started the train this stranger is on!

I was listening to the Dalai Lama last night, on my second bottle of Savvy B, and he said, just because you think someone's a fuckface (okay, he didn't use that exact wording, but you get the picture) doesn't mean they're a fuckface – that's your opinion. Someone else probably thinks that fuckface is a ripper. But if your best friend, who you think is perfect, did something mean to you, your opinion of them would drastically change. Same as if your nemesis started being nice to you, eventually your opinion of them would change. Therefore, there are no fuckfaces or rippers in this world, only perceptions, so don't beat yourself up internally about it, because you're only stressing about your own opinion, and it's a bit up yourself to take it so seriously. So, basically, don't get on the arsehole train for something that is only your opinion. Walk and enjoy yourself instead!

However, when you do end up on the arsehole train (and it will happen from time to time), follow the prick cleanse that I will lay out in chapter 6. Remember that you have the ability to stop the train. Whack the negativity, strip the emotion and view the situation logically. At the end of the day, my girlfriend's boss was just being a bit of an arsewipe, and her hubby just took off his shoes. The chances of being brain damaged or completing community service for assault are pretty low for you

(I hope). But if you reflect on the times you have boarded the train or joined someone else on the train, and recall how the destination of your night/day/event completely changed for the worse, you'll be more motivated to stay off the arsehole train!

DATE YOURSELF

*A*s we get older, we often start saying no to fun, weighed down by our responsibilities as spouses, parents, employees. 'Oh, I'm a mum now, I'd better not.' 'I would have loved to have done that when I was younger, but now I'm too old.' 'I would really love to . . . but I have work in the morning.'

BULLSHIT!

I was talking to a girlfriend of mine last week who felt guilty because we were meeting at a pub for a few drinks. She hadn't been out on a Friday night for over twelve months. When she arrived, she looked stressed. To have this night out she'd had to: organise dinner, bath the kids, read them a book and wait for her daughter (who would only fall asleep with her mum beside her) to doze off before she could make a break for it.

In her mind she felt like she had to pay this 'leave tax' so she could enjoy herself. Why? She said that her husband wouldn't cope if she didn't. Had he said that? NO! Did she tell herself that? Yes! Would she grow to resent the fact that she was doing everything around the house just to have a leave pass? Probably. Was she stripping away or underestimating her husband's identity by assuming he was incapable of making dinner for the kids and doing 100% dad jobs for an evening? YES! Did her husband like her doing these things for him? Of course! I know I would LOVE it if my partner got everything ready before he went out, so I could watch TV on the couch all night.

But what does this overwork achieve apart from boosting her own ego? She does these things because, deep down, she wants to be the one who keeps the house together. She LOVES that her family are reliant on her. Because, realistically, the family won't starve while she's out for a few wines. So what is her intent by running around like a madwoman before her night out, and then telling me about how the family wouldn't survive without her? Self-glorification.

If you're doing this as a mum, what are you teaching your daughters and sons AND partner? Why wouldn't you want your children to see their father actively contributing to running the household, and for your daughter to observe that you can be a mum and keep your own identity?

While I'm using the mum example here, this can apply to anyone who has become defined by the roles they play. Don't get me wrong, you are not a bad person. You are doing the best you can! But somewhere along the line you have sacrificed everything that was once you. So your subconscious is desperately clinging onto whatever it can find to tell you that you are okay. But guess what? You don't need to cook fucking lasagne, wash someone's hair, change your toddler's shitty nappy and help the kids brush their teeth before having a night out to tell yourself you are okay. YOU ARE OKAY! You're better than okay, you're fabulous! But you need to quit the habits that rely on other people's validation to tell yourself this. By practising the techniques in this book, you will fall in love with yourself again and will show your children how to love themselves as well.

Back at the pub, I could see my girlfriend's eyes were exhausted and glassy with tears. She looked around the room, clearly feeling guilty about leaving her family to have fun. Doing what a friend normally does when the chips are low, I indicated for the hot twenty-something bartender to come over. He was a European backpacker type with a man bun, all of his shirt buttons undone so you could see the tribal tattoos underneath that I'm positive he wouldn't know the meaning of. But he gave us a big smile, because at 36 years of age, we were now the old ducks at the bar in need of a bit of attention before we died.

'Two tequila shots please,' I told him, and he gave me a wink.

'Nooooo!' my girlfriend shrieked. 'I have to get up early in the morning!' She looked at me, stressed, as if to say, *I'm hardly coping being here, let alone drinking shots!*

Pedro the bartender (that's not his name but what I've decided to call him in my head) slid us the shots, so I took both of them and downed them one after another. After the second one, I did that gagging thing, where it's 50/50 if you're going to hurl there and then on the bar. I put my hand over my mouth and tucked my chin into my neck until I could gauge whether or not it would rain chunks. But as the tequila spew sensation started to ease, it was replaced by one of the greatest feelings on earth! It's like a storm has finally broken and the sun is creeping back into your guts. I imagine it's very similar to doing CPR on your family dog that's fallen from a balcony (people do that, right?), and he takes a breath and looks into your eyes and you know everything's going to be okay!

As my girlfriend watched me weather the tequila storm, the tension in her face relaxed slightly. A smile came through, her squinting eyes widened, and I could see her as a person, not as a worrying mother and wife.

I asked her, 'Are you okay?'

She looked down at her wine, playing with the stem of the glass, and replied with, 'Fine. I'm just so busy with the kids and work, and my sister is giving us grief about where we are going for Christmas.'

I looked at her again. 'But tell me, are YOU okay?'

She squinted at me again like the tequila had obviously gone to my frontal lobe and caused a mild brain injury. 'You just asked me that,' she replied in a frustrated tone.

'Just tell me, are you okay?' I gave her my *don't try and brush me off* look.

She chuckled as she drank her house Savvy B a little quicker and shuffled around, looking at her phone to check . . . well, nothing, I'd imagine. 'Yes, I'm fine! Stop worrying about me. Tell me, what have you been up to? How are the kids?'

SOUND FAMILIAR? It's pretty much the standard answer from every mum, wife, woman. We have operated in those roles for so long, we honestly cannot tell you how we are going as a person. Because we probably don't know. We haven't spent enough time alone with ourselves for so long, we wouldn't know where to start. Sure, you can tell me how the kids are going, you can tell me about work, we can bitch about a co-worker and that's fun! But try asking yourself these questions: as a person, how are you? What are you feeling? What do YOU want to accomplish this year? What is empowering or enriching your life at the moment? What aren't you enjoying? What are you going to do about it? Now, do your answers start with 'I want to help my son . . .' or 'I want my daughter to achieve . . .'? If they do, these are the wrong answers. I want you to ask yourself the same questions again, but this time your answers must directly benefit you and no one else. Hard, isn't it! It's okay if you can't answer them right now. Plant those seeds in your head and come back to them in a few hours or days, but make sure you do.

Everywhere we go in our lives, we are defined by our titles. Even our deaths are reported by our titles: 'Mother of three Jane Smith didn't survive . . .' It's as if our titles are more significant than our selves. Yes, they're important roles, but YOU AS A PERSON are the base of those roles.

If you were a bed, you as a person would be the mattress. It is the essential foundation of a comfortable bed. Yes, you can add pillows, fancy linen and a throw, and they all help to make a bed great. But if the mattress is not okay, you can dress it up so on the surface everything looks fine, but it will never be truly comfortable.

Now, let's imagine the mattress as a living thing. The mattress wants to make itself a happy, fabulous mattress again, because it wants to feel good. Not necessarily so the person sleeping in it can be comfortable, but because the mattress feels best when its looks after itself. But the mattress feels guilty for wanting to improve its springs, for wanting to be the best mattress it can be. So for years the mattress has accepted being lumpy and sad with shithouse springs as its reality. It has even forgotten its dream of becoming a firm and empowered mattress again. But there's no comfort to be found in a bed without a good mattress, so how could the mattress overlook its importance? It's ludicrous! By not looking after itself, the mattress has not only sacrificed its own happiness, it has made the entire bed less comfortable.

Once the mattress realises this, it finally goes off and gets some new springs. The pillows and throws on top learn by observing the mattress that they too should never settle for being lumpy and sad. The mattress improves and improves, and eventually it's like a brand-new mattress. The pillows are happier because they have a strong stable base to lie on. The throws feel fantastic and more secure, because the bed is proud of itself and empowered to be the best mattress it can be, therefore being a much better base for everything else. Now it is a comfortable, fully rounded bed that benefits everyone.

So don't be the sad and lumpy mattress, okay? You are the base of all of your titles, and you need to service this base regularly. Chances are you've forgotten what you like or what fuels your soul. This doesn't mean you are completely lost! It just means you must get to know yourself again. Lots has probably happened since you've hung out alone with yourself. Take yourself out on a date. Where are you going to go?

*

When I asked myself out on a date, I chose water aerobics. I'd never been before and, to be honest, I'd never thought about going. But it was something just for me, and it was something completely unrelated to the roles in my life. I looked up the local gym timetable and saw it was on Saturdays at 9 am. Perfect.

When Saturday rolled around, I woke to the constant nagging of 'Muuuuuuuuum,' like every Saturday morning. I asked the kids what they wanted for breakfast as they stared like zombies at the TV with bed knots in the back of their hair. No reply from my three-year-old daughter, Matilda, or my five-year-old son, Freddie, so I asked again like some kind of desperate feeding housewife. No fucking answer.

'Okay, go hungry,' I muttered as I turned the kettle on to make a coffee.

Which was when they both miraculously regained their hearing (thank the lord, it's a miracle!) and replied with 'Paaaaaaaaaancakes,' their eyes not leaving the TV.

Of course you do, I thought to myself as I walked towards the fridge to grab the eggs and milk. *God forbid you'd want something simple. I'll just crack these, stir this, get the lumps out, get the frying pan and chuck them on, shall I?*

Norm stumbled out of the bedroom in a pair of white and blue jocks (the ones with the hole in the left butt cheek), one eye bigger than the other after having too many beers at the bowls club the night before.

'Big night last night, hun?' I asked him as I cracked the second egg into the bowl of flour.

'No, not really,' he responded, 'just a few quiet ones with the boys.' He wearily walked into the kitchen and unscrewed the jar of Moccona.

'So, anything exciting happen last night?' I asked.

'No, just a few quiet ones,' he said again. He raised his elbow to pour the milk into his Collingwood premiership cup, and a nuclear bomb of sweat and alcohol infected my nose.

He walked outside to the verandah to sit in his usual spot, a green leather recliner that stinks and has yellow foam exploding from its torn right arm. He refuses to throw it out. He reckons it's his thinking chair, but I haven't seen him come up with many good ideas after sitting in it. It has a cup holder on one side that fits his XXXX can perfectly. He says the chair is one of his best mates: 'Who else holds your can for you without asking for anything in return?' Anyway, as he walked to his verandah seat, his waft loyally travelled with him.

What he didn't realise is there is no greater detective than a woman home alone with the kids on a Friday night. When I hadn't been able to contact him at 11 pm the night before, I'd obviously thought he was dead. So I wasn't snooping but easing my anxiety about his potential passing when I logged onto his NetBank account. I mean, on reflection, I could have called the bowls club, but in the moment logging onto his NetBank seemed like the only way to be sure he was still alive. And there it was: I counted the transactions on his statement and he had been to the bar eighteen times. Not that there was any reason for me to be resentful or angry. This is the most important part! If we are reclaiming our identities and souls, we have to have the same respect for our partners. If drinking eighteen beers at the bowls club is their journey to happiness, so be it. If Norm wants to be hungover while I'm out of the house, that's his call. My partner's actions will no longer trigger my guilt as a mother or wife.

Let me explain: it is very common in this situation to feel guilt or anxiety that your partner's at the pub. You tell yourself you won't be able to do water aerobics, because he will be too hungover, so you will be left with the kids and never get to do anything for yourself. How could he be so irresponsible by doing this to you? He doesn't care for you; he doesn't love you. I'm telling you now, QUIT THAT! You're creating a situation in your mind that doesn't exist. I know these thoughts come from a place of love. You don't want him to feel sick or hungover when he's looking after the children. But guess what? He is an adult, he knows you won't be home tomorrow and that's what he chooses to do. There's nothing wrong with that. You cannot protect your family from every piece of pain and hurt. Let go of trying to control others, because it will free up copious amounts of energy to regain the control of your own life.

Having finished flipping the pancakes, I yelled out, 'Kiiiiiiiiiids, breakfast is ready.' They ignored me again because *Dora the Explorer* was on, so I used my louder mum voice. 'Breeeeeakfast now!'

They ran to the table and started fighting over the same freaking chair.

'Muuuuuuuuuuuuuuuuuum, Matilda's got my chair!' Freddie whined as Matilda kicked him in the ribs with a huge smile on her face. I would imagine this chair victory would feel similar to an Olympic medal for a three-year-old.

'Sit on the other chair, Fred. No one owns chairs!' I replied as I presented a dish of shitty, half-burnt, misshapen pancakes and toast.

'I bet Santa owns chairs!' came my son's reply, accompanied by a kick to his sister under the table.

I had a third attempt at making myself a cup of coffee, and this time I got the teaspoon of coffee in the cup before my daughter looked at me and screamed,

'Muuuuuuuuuum, my toast is touching my pancakes. I need new ones!' A huge snot bubble inflated from her left nostril like a birthday balloon.

My son started crying in turn because he'd decided he didn't like pancakes anymore and wanted lollies for breakfast. But rather then tell me like a normal person, he did that WHINE. You know, that soul-destroying 'Muuuuuuuuuuuuuuuuuuuurm.' I swear they should play that noise over and over again to our enemies at war. Three minutes in a room with 'Muuuuuuuuuuuurm Muuuuuuuuuuuurm Muuuuuuuuuuuurm', and they'd spill all of their secrets like a wet rag and beg for mercy!

(By the way, wine and whine create two polar opposite effects in the brain. When the land of word makers were sitting around the table, they opened up the file to 'freaking annoying elongated high-pitched sound that a child makes at any time of the day for any reason'. What should we call this? Okay! Let's take a delicious drink that is often used for medicinal purposes after long exposure to this sound and chuck a silent H in it.)

I looked at my watch and saw it was 8.30. My snot-ridden daughter let out another scream while stamping her left foot on the scratched floorboards. It's hard to take anyone seriously when they're wearing a Peppa Pig dress on top of an Emma Wiggle dress on top of one-piece bathers, with pink and yellow goggles resting on their nose like reading glasses. 'Muuuuuuuuum, new toast!'

'Sorry, you'll have to ask Dad. I have to go!' I said, suddenly delighted as I realised none of this was my problem. The kids looked at me like I was the Red Cross pulling all rations and healthcare from their refugee camp. They were genuinely perplexed at the thought of me doing something for myself. This wasn't their fault, because I had created this habit for all of us. But guess what? New me, new habits!

I popped my head out the door and said to Norm with a huge smile on my face, 'I've gotta go to aerobics. Wish me luck, love ya!'

See my sign-off there? It's clear, simple and precise. You're doing this for you; you're not playing games. So sign-offs like 'Have fun', 'They're your problem now' or 'Good luck' allude to you getting one back at your partner or leaving him with a stressful situation. But doing something for yourself is the new normal for your family, so try to avoid turning it into a chore for your partner. To create positive change, you need to use positive energy. I'll talk more about this in the next chapter, when we do our prick cleanse.

As I drove out of the driveway, I felt a wave of excitement! I hadn't done anything for myself since before we'd had children! What was this fabulous world I'd been missing out on?

I found myself smiling in my one-piece bathing suit, walking down the side of the outdoor pool at the local gym. An elderly lady with a purple bathing suit, a matching hat and a full face of makeup was already in the pool and warning the ladies around her not to splash her hair, because she'd just washed it and she had to go to the butchers after this. The instructor gave me a smile and pointed me to a council wheelie bin full of pool noodles and foam dumbbells. I walked back towards the pool, not realising until afterwards that my pubes were sprawling out the sides of my bathers like the grass reshooting after the bushfires at Russell Crowe's farm. The sun was beaming down on us, so I can only imagine how the majestic glisten of my pubic hair caught the eyes of my new-found friends.

But I had made it here, and so have you. We are quitting an expectation that our family needs us to do everything for them. We are quitting the need to boost our ego by thinking our family would be doomed without us. We are not going to control what others do, instead we are going to accept them for having and living their own identity, just as you are. We are going to accept that we need to get to know ourselves again. Changing that behaviour might be scary but it is vital!

It's time to ask yourself those questions again, and remember, you must answer only for yourself. And I won't accept an answer that includes, 'Well, my children enrich my life, so I am allowed to include their achievements?' This is just YOU. Imagine you're sitting across the table from yourself, and ask:

How are you?

What are you feeling?

What do YOU want to accomplish this year?

What is empowering or enriching your life at the moment?

What aren't you as a person enjoying?

What are you going to do about it?

And here's a bonus question:

What's something you've always wanted to do but haven't done yet?

Once you have an answer for this bonus question, do it! BOOK IT IN NOW! Even if you don't feel ready, just book it! Why wouldn't ya? I'm begging you, make that first step now. It might be something small, but it starts the ball rolling. Seriously, this is a book, you aren't going to miss anything. Put the book down, set up something you've always wanted to do and come back.

Oh, what's that? You're just reading on instead? Chances are you've told yourself one of these things:

- I can't afford it.

- I'll do it another time, like later or tomorrow.

- I'll just read the next chapter first.

- All of the above, or some other bullshit excuse.

If you said, 'I can't afford it,' I hate to break it to you but change doesn't cost money. If that was the case, only rich people would ever change their habits. Now, if you always wanted to go bungee-jumping or skydiving, I get the point that you may not have enough in the account for that. But it's not about the activity, it's about the intention of doing something for you. You might be saying, 'Well, all I really want to do is go skydiving' (or supplement sky diving with any other activity you want to do but can't because of time/money/location). Let's get this straight. THE ONLY THING IN THE WORLD THAT IS GOING TO RECLAIM YOUR LOST IDENTITY IS THIS UNATTAINABLE ACTIVITY?! So because you cannot do that specific activity right now, you're destined to a life without fulfilment?

Let's do a little exercise. Say this out loud: 'Jess wanted

a fulfilled life but when she couldn't afford to skydive, she decided to quit working towards happiness and lived the rest of her life frustrated and unfulfilled.' Sounds ridiculous, doesn't it? But if you haven't put this book down and organised something for yourself, then you sound like Jess.

Now go. Book it! Organise it! It won't take long. But whatever it is, go on your own, at least the first time. You're starting new habits and thought patterns. Old conversations could trigger old thoughts.

Let's pretend we're at the bar together and we're brainstorming what you should do. You go first.

- ....

- ....

- ....

- ....

- ....

Yep, I love those ideas! Here's a few from me.

- Zumba

- Pottery

- Yoga (It's easier than I thought it would be, especially if you start off with relaxation yoga, where you don't even break a sweat.)

- A freaking walk by yourself (TOTALLY FREE!)

- Joining a team for a sport you've never done before, like basketball or social tennis (Oh, you don't want to look stupid because you've never done it before? What would you tell your children if they said that to you on their first day of sports practice? Well, tell yourself that right now! Plus, there'll be other people there who've never done it either. Are you calling them stupid? Quit it! New you, remember?)

- Painting class

If you really can't think of anything you want to do, I'll make the decision for you. YOGA! Book now, there are free intro sessions everywhere.

You've taken the first step on the path to remembering what's great about you the person. So proud of ya!

6
DO THE PRICK CLEANSE

It's time to give yourself a mental enema. Let's flush out all the toxins. This will be the most important cleanse you'll ever do in your life. We talk about gut cleanses, diets, meal plans and personal trainers as tools to shape our bodies. (Personally, I've never found them useful and have instead shaped my body into a perfectly round ball that can roll down hills at the speed of light.) Yet the most important thing we can shape is our minds.

The fitness marketing industry preaches 'a healthy body equals a healthy mind'. What a load of crap. Are you telling me everyone who is carrying a sixpack and a nice arse has a healthy mind? Healthy people are some of the most fucked-up people I know, same with unhealthy people. We are all fucked up! So don't pigeonhole us cellulite-ridden folk as unhappy individuals. We are all in this together, forced to face a world of disaster, pain and suffering. Yet we are also all in this together, capable of embracing a world of heroism, motivation, love and respect.

Yes, being physically healthy is great for you and does generally make you feel better mentally, but you haven't changed the way you think or created neurological muscle memory. You've simply given yourself a task and worked towards it (life with purpose always feels good), creating some feel-good endorphins along the way. So right now, when you're exercising you feel great. But what if your life turns to shit? What if something really upsets you? You haven't built the mental strength to deal with that like you have developed the physical strength to lift a weight.

Everything you are right now, everything you have achieved, is linked to your train of thought and the habits you create for yourself. YOUR MIND IS EVERYTHING! It's your universe and the one thing you can't escape. If you were told you would be trapped in the same house until you died, would you want it to be an unpleasant and uncomfortable environment? Or would you prefer it to be decked out with all the luxuries to give you the best life possible? Of course you would be asking for the greatest comforts the universe could provide. Well, baby cakes, your mind is your castle, and together we are going make it the comfiest fucking castle you have ever stepped into.

✱

What if you could cleanse your mind of negative thinking? What if you could shape your mind as simply as you shape your body? You can! And in the process, you can free up most of your emotional energy to reinvest in yourself.

This cleanse was inspired by the 'Seven day mental diet', a pamphlet I found lying next to some magazines at the laundromat in a caravan park when we were on holidays (and which, it turns out, is also a book by Emmet Fox. Who knew?). Actively practising it has changed my life and the lives of others I've told about it.

Unlike with a physical cleanse, keeping a positive mentality is invisible. There's no evidence we can touch or hold to keep us in line. So we are going to need complete honesty with ourselves. If we liken this to a renovation, right now we are doing the demolition. We will clear up and throw out all of the old crap that has bothered you, so you can start fresh. You are the only person who can create a great life for yourself, so before we start I need you to stop justifying your lack of progress, happiness, fullfilment or just a happy soul on an external reason/situation/person/event. Unless you want to become President of the United States without having been born there, the only thing holding you back from what you'd like to do is yourself. Let's start working on you.

For the next seven days, you will not entertain any negative thoughts that pop into your mind. Think of them as weeds that you see in the garden and pull them out straight away. This includes our negative judgements of others, whether on social media or TV, in magazines or real-life encounters, because when we judge others, subconsciously we are filling an egotistical need through a negative emotion, which will breed further negativity within you.

If you absorb someone else's behaviour, whether it's a memory or a current situation, and think, *What an idiot*, immediately whack it out of your head! Thinking that a person is a fuckwit might justify your anger and feel good in the moment, but it's putting you into a negative emotional space. And you're emotionally quitting and cleansing pricks, remember? WHACK IT! Think to yourself, *Not my problem*, and go back to whatever you were thinking about prior to that (*What am I cooking tonight? What am I doing tomorrow?*). That person or event now holds no emotion for you and you need to maintain that mindset.

You are no better than anyone else and nobody is better than you. The perception of status is driven by ego or insecurity. Whether it's the guy cleaning out the public toilets or the surgeon performing heart surgery on your loved one, each person deserves your compassion and respect. Transform your inner narrative of *What a loser* or *Get a real job* into *What a great worker* or *He looks like he takes pride in his work; good on him*. Keeping these inner narratives positive is vital to the cleanse.

I'm not saying you need to avoid all news reports of negative events happening in the world. It is okay to absorb this information, but don't prolong your thought pattern about how bad the world is. If we see an article about war, a virus, the plague, we tend to go into a 'the world's stuffed and my children are going to die' emotional black hole. Whenever you find yourself catastrophising your world, STOP and whack it! I know you're an amazing person, but you are not responsible for war. It's sad and it's horrible, but whether you lose a day freaking out or you gain a day living happily in your world, you won't affect the outcome of that war. So whack it!

Oh, and stop watching videos of children dying or people getting hurt. You know exactly what that video is about; your brain is screwing you over royally to get its negative fix. Once you realise what's happening, you become responsible for your actions. Why would you click yes to a video you know is going to make you sad? There's no freaking need in this universe for you to click play, except for your prick-addicted need to get a negative fix.

Make sure you're whacking any insecure thoughts of yourself, whether inflicted internally or externally. As soon as any self-deprecating thoughts pop in your head, throw them out immediately.

When someone's being negative, you don't need to cut them off, preach to them or leave. Let them have their say, but don't let their perception of life become yours. You can offer solutions or be a listening ear, but the minute you start to take on their shit, you need to pull that weed out of your mind.

Naturally, negative thoughts are going to keep popping into your head, but you have granted yourself a reprieve from them for the next seven days. Say you're at work and the boss says something that spirals you into an *Am I good enough?* or *What a prick* whirlwind, STOP! Remind yourself that you are on a cleanse and refocus on the original task at hand. Smack it away, like a fly on your sausage roll in the middle of summer. It means nothing to you. If it comes back, just keep smacking it.

When you start this cleanse, you'll think, *For fuck's sake, everything's going wrong.* But it's not. Two things are happening. One, you're consciously identifying your negative thought patterns. And two, you are being tested, which happens with anything that's worth achieving. Basically, if it makes you feel bad, whack it. You'll still have to deal with your everyday problems, but by whacking the emotional negativity, you can choose to approach situations logically as opposed to emotionally. It will probably take a couple of goes at first, but just whack and reset, whack and reset.

If you tested positive to being a prick addict back in chapter 1, this approach is like going cold turkey for drug addicts. It's rehab, but you don't have to wear one of those gowns that shows your butt cheeks. It won't be easy. When I initially started this cleanse, I forgot I was about to enter into a hormone cycle that resembled Cyclone Yasi, the weather patterns forecasting mass destruction for myself and my family. The first two days were the calm before the storm. I felt refreshed and awoken, bounding off the pavement as I walked, feeling like I had cracked the code. I loved my family, I loved my partner, I loved my work, and no amount of fuck-wittery was going to knock me off my peaceful path to a world with no bullshit.

I don't know if it was the hormones, the three-day relapse, work, the moon or my ovaries, but on the third day I looked like Hitler reincarnated. I was FURIOUS! I tried to whack. I whacked so hard I would have knocked Mike Tyson out in the first round and bitten both his ears off, feeding them to the seagulls at Noosa beach with an evil smirk on my face. But the emotion of anger towards everything in my life was surging in like the 2011 Brisbane floods, and everything I'd worked so hard at was being washed away!

We have a moodle called Denise. She's tan and small and gorgeous. I sat next to her on the couch and she gazed into my eyes with that look of love and nurture, knowing something wasn't right. I stared back into her brown heart-melting eyes with long eyelashes and said, 'What the fuck are you looking at, Denise? FUCK OFF!'

She stood up and jumped off the couch, probably thinking, *This bitch crazy.*

I kept saying to myself, 'Whack it, whack it, whack it, whack it!' But the power of negativity was too strong. I really was a prick addict and I was going through bad withdrawals. My mind was flooded with memories of being hard done by in every facet of my life, and the internal narrative of justification was saying to me, *But you are allowed to think about these moments because they weren't your fault. Remember when that person at work yelled at you in 2005? You didn't deserve that!* Yet what was dwelling on that going to achieve in my life? I was only wallowing in the past of no solutions.

I started to believe my own internal narrative and took out my phone to read every text conversation I'd had with a work colleague for the previous sixteen months. The angry texts reinforced my inner narrative, while I viewed the positive texts without gratitude, treating them as condescending behaviour. My mind even manipulated a text that said *great job today, love everything you do, have a great weekend* to read as sarcastic.

My prick addiction was ruining every experience in my life. If being addicted to negativity was ice, I was having a full relapse, probably walking naked down the highway, wearing a tiara, telling people I used to have a million-dollar tech company but I lost it in the financial crash, and if you could give me a dollar, I'd promise to give it back to you when I got back on my feet. I was reaching at anything and everything to nurture the prick habit I'd created over twenty years.

My thoughts were broken by a call from a school mum who I knew would want to go for coffee. I ignored it because my head had no room for anything but my own thoughts. My prick addiction knew that if I went to have coffee, it wouldn't be able to control everything happening in my mind. My house of negative emotion, which had been falling into ruins, was suddenly being upgraded, and the clients had ordered the freaking spa. That house was starting to look like the Taj Mahal, and as the sole builder, I couldn't afford to take time off for coffee.

I knew I'd relapsed, so I took the day off the prick cleanse, knowing I had to restart it the next day from day one. I still tried to internally whack those negative thoughts a little, just to save myself from plummeting into the seventh stage of depression. I surprised myself with my natural whacking ability and how even in my time of rock bottom, I could still find the urge to whack those thoughts.

If you don't go through the day three relapse, amazing! You might not be as addicted as I was, you might just be better at whacking negative thoughts, or you might be using this exercise to improve yourself rather than break an addiction. But if you do relapse, know that this is not something to be ashamed of. It means that you are actively taking steps to improve your life, which is a great thing. We are in this together. Remember, how you feel when you relapse is how you used to feel every day. You are just aware of it now. Can you imagine living your whole life in that negative spiral, and not having a road map to get out of it? How you were before starting the cleanse is far more scary, because you thought those feelings were normal. Ultimately, a relapse day will probably not feel worse than you have felt in the past. Yet because you have lived a few positive days in the meantime, the contrast between the two moods will be striking.

So let's pick ourselves up, reset, take the day off and start again tomorrow. When you wake up, remind yourself that you know exactly what you need to do. You have the map. It doesn't matter if you get lost 50 times, your life will be better because you're on this journey.

Think of this technique as how you would deal with an ember from a fire. Imagine you are sitting in your favourite hoody and a pair of shorts next to an open fireplace, wine and tacos in hand, when an ember flies up and lands on your hand. You could flick it off straight away, no harm done. Or you could jump up and run around the room panicking that the ember will burn you, before you finally hear your friend yelling at you to FLICK IT OFF, so you do. You will now have a deeper wound to heal. This wound will annoy you for days, following you everywhere you go. Now, think of the embers as your thoughts. Don't panic when they land on you, just flick them off and go about your day.

When I went on this cleanse, it felt like spiritual valium to rid myself of my internal negative controller. If I embarrassed myself after too many drinks on Saturday night, I wasn't allowed to feel guilty or worry that my friends hated or judged me. Oh, what sweet lawless international waters had we landed in? This new-found freedom was what it must have felt like in *The Shawshank Redemption* when the main character dug the hole in the wall and crawled through the tunnel to end up living at the beach! The freedom of having a fantastic night on the wine, and not worrying later about what we said or did, is one that you and I can now enjoy.

The worry and anxiety still knock on the door of my consciousness, screaming at me to let them in, because they still have the old neurological pathways to walk down. Yet every time they knock, I open the door and whack them, which means we are winning the cleanse. Your mirror will now be your trophy cabinet to celebrate your huge smile and sparkling eyes every day!

Don't tell anyone you're doing the cleanse until you've finished it. Store up all your energy to heal yourself. Once you're done, you'll shout it from the rooftops, because you'll realise how profoundly it has changed your life. However, right now, keep your focus on you and only you.

Let's deal with the situation of doing this cleanse when you have a significant negative force in your daily life. What if they say or do something mean to you? That is an act carried out by them, out of their own negative thinking. They're not on the same path as you. Whatever emotion that makes you feel, whack it! Don't get frustrated at them or pity them; you need to save your energy for the cleanse. Go back and read chapter 1, and emotionally quit that prick.

See this situation as a test for your cleanse. Your angry or insecure emotion is going to feel right at home, because it's been visiting you for years, but as soon as you see it dumping its suitcase on the spare bed, whack it! You might have two seconds of peace before it pops up again – whack! – then you might get seven seconds this time before you feel it creep back and have to whack it all over again.

You aren't failing if the negative emotion keeps coming back. Your mind has been trying to fuck you up since you were born, and you won't be able to stop that. What we are working on is strengthening your whacking arm. Your brain will try to trick you into thinking that the negative emotion deserves to live in your mind, it's comfortable in your mind, it's just easier, and your emotion is so big that nobody would be able to whack it away. Bullshit! Get yourself up, dust yourself off. You wouldn't be reading this book if you didn't want to improve your quality of life. In this moment you're like one of the *Biggest Loser* contestants who are sweaty and crying on the floor, with the trainers screaming, 'ONE MORE!' And guess what? They do one more. And guess what else? They lose a shit ton of weight and live an extra twenty years. Whenever you start thinking it's easier to marinate yourself in the shit sauce of life, it's not, you're just giving in.

That negative someone in your life might not even be saying something directly to you, but their body language might bring up a negative feeling in you. Obviously the same rules apply. WHACK IT! Reset and go back to your original task.

Remember when we talked about negative narcissism in chapter 2, where you might feel responsible for other people's bad moods? Understand this: other people aren't carnival rides where they are paid to make you feel happy. They have their own shit going on, and this cleanse is about you, not them. You also aren't responsible for other people's happiness; they need to find it just like you do. If someone is drowning in a pool of negativity, you will help them far more by throwing them a lifebuoy from your sunbed of positivity than letting them pull you under the water.

That person's bad mood could be because of something you did or said, of course, and if it is, you'll need to deal with that in a logical manner. This cleanse isn't about avoiding problems, getting naked and blowing on a dandelion. This cleanse is about not letting negative thoughts consume your life. Ask that person if they are okay. If they say no, find out the problem and deal with it. If they say yes, the emotional responsibility of resolving it transfers to them, and you are once again free to whack all thoughts of *But what if they . . .* Confront a personal problem like you'd confront a problem with your car. Address it, resolve it, whack any negative thoughts that pop up about it. How good's livin'? You just bought yourself freedom, my friend.

We often say we've had a bad day, but unless you're ridiculously unlucky, the chances of everything in your day going wrong are pretty small. That's why we need to whack the negative thoughts as soon as we spot them, limiting them to one bad minute and not letting them ruin our day. This is the purpose of the cleanse. FOR THE LOVE OF GOD, WHACK IT NOW BEFORE IT SPREADS!

✷

Here's an example of what a difference the cleanse can make. A girlfriend of mine bought her mum an Apple Watch only to find out her mum already had one. So she was already annoyed because her mum hadn't told her she'd bought a watch. She then asked her mum to send the watch back to her, as they lived 1000 kilometres apart, so my friend could get a refund and buy her mum something else. When her mum dropped the watch off at the post office, she specifically bought the type of postage that needed to be signed for. It was a $350 watch, so they didn't want to risk it being stolen.

Four days later the watch arrived at my girlfriend's place. However, the postie left it by the door, undercover, instead of asking her to sign for it. The watch was in perfect condition when my girlfriend found it there, but she was furious that it could have been stolen. She was angry at the laziness of the postie and angry at the post office for taking the extra $3.50 for the registered parcel when it wasn't treated like one. She rang the post office and demanded answers about her abandoned parcel. She was on hold for 75 minutes while she was transferred from department to department. They said they would look into it further (I suspect to get her off the phone) and email her with a case report.

The parcel had been delivered at 8 am; it was now midday, and she was still furious. The watch was fine, nothing in her life would have physically changed if it was signed for or not. Yet because she didn't whack her negative thought when it reared its ugly head, she let it grow like a weed and consume her. Something as simple as a parcel delivery had robbed her of four hours she would never get back. Her frustration threw her into a negative mindset where she viewed the rest of the world as being as incompetent as the postie. She carried that same judgement through to her partner when he got home, so they had a fight. She downed two bottles of wine, started crying and went to bed at 6 pm. She woke up at 3 am with a dry mouth, a headache, an unfinished presentation for her work and a complicated relationship. ALL BECAUSE OF THE FUCKING PARCEL!

Now, let's view this case study through the cleanse method. It's a much shorter story.

- 8.00 am: Was expecting to sign for a parcel.

- 8.01 am: Realised the postie had left it on the verandah, checked it and the watch was fine.

- 8.02 am: Whacked any negative emotions that came up about the postie and went on to have a great day.

This is the drastic difference the cleanse could make to your life. And you can start practising it today!

When you apply these techniques, your focus will shift from 'this happened to me' to 'I made this happen'. Understand that it's a huge commitment, so don't take it lightly. But the rewards are exponential and there's nothing stopping you from starting. You don't need to buy a membership; you don't need to buy a yoga mat. If you feel like this is your time, you can start right now! This is your journey, but you aren't alone because many have done this cleanse before you. Many are probably starting today as they read the exact page you're reading now.

Your life will undoubtedly change in the next seven days, or whenever you choose to achieve the cleanse. However, the brain is a muscle and needs work (just like personal training) to maintain your practice of positive thought, so I recommend doing the seven-day cleanse for one week of every month. You'll find some months easier or harder than others. However, just like with physical fitness, you won't realise you have deteriorated a little until you hit the gym again.

Now, don't forget, on each of the seven days of the cleanse, whack every negative thought whenever it creeps into your consciousness. Repeat for one week every month.

If you relapse, it's okay! You're doing some pretty big restructuring in your mind. Shake it off and start again tomorrow. Remember how you feel today as evidence of how you don't want to live.

And finally, here's an interesting fact for you. When I whack my emotions, for some reason I would swipe them to the left like they were being thrown in a pool. I've since discovered that our positivity comes from the left-hand side of the brain. So when something negative creeps in, try whacking it to the left. You've got this!

FIND YOUR
WORTH AT
WORK

*W*ork can be like a prick salad, full of limp carrots, bitter lettuce and sour tomatoes. You are surrounded by people who have no emotional attachment to your wellbeing whatsoever. But that's work! A whole bunch of personalities, with their own agendas and inner pricks manifesting, trying to work together in an office without killing each other. Top it off with a birthday cake for every fucking birthday, as you fake smile and sing to a guy who we know told Suzy at the dishwasher that you were fat.

If this wasn't enough hell, they make you do team bonding exercises. Fall back into the arms of your handsy colleague, his hands getting close enough to your breasts for a complaint to HR. You awkwardly stand up, feeling the dawning guilt of your 3 pm deadline for an Excel spreadsheet, while your boss thinks she's New Age because she bought some name tags and a snack platter and hired a guy called Derek to say you all need to work as a team. Or you're taken to paintball, where Garry from Accounts exposes his inner psycho and shoots not only the opposing team but also his own as he lives out his fantasy of massacring the entire office. Your office might appear harmonious for the next couple of days, but in fact it's the horror of the bonding session distracting everyone from their miserable lives, and you all go back to hating one another within the week.

An office will generally include the team players who genuinely want everyone to work together to achieve a common goal, the ones who don't care about the team but want to share in the accolades, those who thrive by bringing others down, those who are brilliant but too beaten down by life to realise it, and the ones who are more focused on what Tiffany's doing in sales than their own work. So many different personalities, each with their own inner prick, who's developed over the years from their unique traumatic events.

It's like being in spiritual hell at times, with emotional thieves and ego-slayers everywhere you look. But you can't leave, because you need to pay the rent! You're a prisoner in your own head. You've dreamed of opening your own business and being free. Yet do you actually want to run your own business, or do you just want to choose who you surround yourself with, to not feel at the mercy of the boss's opinion of you? If you're the boss, nobody can tell you that you aren't doing a good job, right? But while you fantasise endlessly about it, you never take the plunge because you have bills to pay and financially it could be too risky and you can't really be bothered starting a business right now. Which are all excuses for not following your dreams because you don't have the confidence.

If you were strong enough to chase your destiny, then you'd be strong enough not to listen to the prick salad around you. You would realise your worth and be able to make decisions that are not blinded by emotion or driven by your inner prick. You wouldn't be listening to bloody Cheryl, the 2IC, who's feeling worthless after a marriage breakup and, rather than getting her hands dirty by exploring the origin of her inner prick, has decided to steal your emotional coins to buy her own happiness. (You need to emotionally quit Cheryl now. Go back to chapter 1 and work it through.)

You go back to your desk and look over at your boss. She might be having a bad day because she's boarded someone's arsehole train and is now doing everything she can to recruit you as a passenger. However, unlike the arsehole train of a random person on the street, seeing a boss's arsehole train steaming towards you shatters your illusions of job security. All of a sudden, you're visualising being sacked, on welfare and shaking your fanny for dollars, only now you're too old to be high end so must embrace being a fetish like a milf or a 'larger lady'. Your boss's arsehole train turns you into a negative narcissist, where the entire universe revolves around you, and she's definitely in a mood because she didn't like the PowerPoint presentation you sent her yesterday.

You have let the entire office of personalities affect your emotional stability and self-worth. You have left your emotional doors wide open, pretty much saying, 'Hey, why don't you come in and rob me of everything?'

You go home and talk to you partner about work for hours, reliving the traumatic experience of your day over and over. We spoke in the introduction about spending your emotional coins, but let me show you again:

- Pissed off by boss at 9.05 am during a twelve-minute meeting.

- Thought about pissed-off moment for two hours after meeting ended.

- Rang friend at lunch to talk for 25 minutes about how the boss is a dickhead.

- Spent three more hours at work reliving other annoying things the boss has done.

- Came home and ranted to housemate/partner for one more hour about boss.

- Rang Mum and ranted for one more hour about boss.

- Could not sleep for four hours while thinking about how much I hate my boss.

So, your meeting went for twelve minutes, but you spent eleven hours and 25 minutes dwelling on it and creating negative habits for yourself that are going to take weeks to undo.

You also didn't get any work done today, which is a lost opportunity given that progressing or accomplishing something is the food to build confidence within yourself.

When the next day arrives, your boss says good morning and gives you a compliment. All is back to normal there. But the new negative neurological habits you created yesterday will want to be actively fed from any source they can find.

You blame the job because it does not give you enough emotional energy to spend with your family, focus on your goals or allow yourself to feel good. It's all work's fault! You need to leave. If you left, you would play with your kids or spoil your partner or start making pottery, because you'd be in a better headspace to accomplish what you want in life rather than worrying about what's happening in the office.

Unfortunately, that's bullshit. I know, devastating! I too would like to blame all my internal issues on my surroundings; it would be so much easier. However, using this strategy, you'd have more chance of obtaining peace and happiness from a durry butt at the bottom of a Coke bottle you find at a park. We are the drivers of our own destiny, remember? We are the only ones who have control over the inner narrative of our lives. We can't rely on the actions of others to fulfil us. This reliance feels good sometimes, when things are going well, but when they're going badly, it's horrible, uncontrollable and unsustainable.

The good news is, as annoying as your work environment might be, it's the perfect environment to develop the skills to find your worth and be confident. If you can emotionally quit pricks and focus on your worth in this environment, you are going to blossom in an environment that nurtures and loves you. However, if you run from this environment (generally at the sacrifice of your own career) and find something kinder, you will never develop these skills with the same intensity. If quitting was the path to emotional enlightenment, people who hand in resignation letters because they're unhappy at work should theoretically be enlightened the moment they walk out the office doors. But how many times have you seen someone quit their job because they thought it was the root of all their problems, yet the unhappiness followed them? Fuck a duck! It's almost like unhappiness was a habit they developed, and although the external environment may have triggered their misery, the way work made them feel was an exaggerated version of a story they had been telling themselves internally for years.

Inner narratives of ourselves are a bit like cold sores: they're always bubbling beneath the surface. One day, an external event might happen and BANG, there it is, like a fried egg on your face. What I'm about to tell you is a bullshit analogy, because there's no cure for cold sores, but for the sake of the analogy let's just pretend there is one, because I can't think of another analogy right now, and as I write this in our back shed four metres away from the house, where I'm getting away from the kids to write, I can hear my daughter screaming, 'Muuuuuuuuuuuuuuuuuuum . . . bottttttttttttttle!' and I'm screaming back, 'Nooooooooooooooooooorm, I'm writing! Get Matilda a bottttttttle,' and he's screaming, 'Where is onnnnnnnnne?' and I'm screaming, 'In the fuckkkkkkkking bottle drawer, where else?' and he's screaming, 'Alright no need to sweeeeeeeeeeeear,' and I'm screaming, 'Im notttt fucking swearinnnnnnnnng,' and then my daughter is screaming, 'Bottttttttttttttttt-tttttttttttttttttle!' and then I'm questioning myself as a mother, because should she still be drinking from a bottle if she can perfectly articulate 'botttttttttttttle'?

My prick addiction is flaring up, because the anger of Norm not knowing where the fucking bottles are is infuriating! If he gave Matilda more bottles, he'd know where they are. He needs to be home more. Plus he needs to start taking the change out of his pockets when I do the washing. Is it that freaking hard? Breathe, Jess, breathe! Don't entertain the negative thoughts, prick cleanse it, inhale, whack it, exhale, okay . . . So, for the love of god, just go along with 'there's a cure for cold sores', okay?

Inner narratives of ourselves are a bit like cold sores, they're always bubbling beneath the surface. One day an external event might happen and BANG, there it is, like a fried egg on your face. However, if you went straight to the source of the cold sore, you would invest the time in curing it rather than just rubbing cream on it when it was already exposed and too late. Quitting your job or running from a situation is like putting cream on a cold sore. It'll do the trick short term, but eventually the destructive habits you have taught yourself will bubble up and need to be cured.

So right now, you're in one of the most valuable positions to change the way you think for the rest of your life. You're surrounded by pricks, you leave work feeling like your worth has been stolen and you're unvalued. What a great training ground to start emotionally quitting the way people make you feel. It's like you're at the

Cunt Olympics! If you were surrounded by nice, loving and supportive people, you would not be able to actively practise these techniques, thus they wouldn't be as strong. Use that as your gratitude.

Don't expect to go to work tomorrow and nail it. We have neurological pathways to build, habits to create, discipline to hold ourselves to. But there's one thing we have that we didn't have yesterday, and that's a plan. A plan to progress ourselves psychologically and professionally. We've got this. Truly, we do! Don't let the opinions of others affect the way we work or our performance. Don't let someone else's story of us be ours. Write your own destiny, stop giving someone else the fucking pen!

✗

Let's deal with one of the most common frustrations in a workplace: someone has been promoted over you or achieved more because they're friends with the boss or success maker. You think, *They're useless!* They don't deserve what they have achieved and it drives you crazy. But guess what? They still deserved it. Why? Because they might not be as skilled at the job as you, but that person has identified what that boss wants emotionally to think they are the best person for the job. They worked hard creating and nurturing a relationship. Their skill is with their social intelligence and ability to read the boss's psyche. AND IT DRIVES US CRAZY! But it works.

I worked with a guy like this years ago, and for the sake of not getting sued I'll call him Daniel. Daniel was my manager at a call centre, and he and the big boss had become great friends while Daniel was working directly for him, with the two of them going out for drinks often. Daniel was earning around $150K a year. The rest of us were making $23 an hour on a casual wage, with a bonus $5 per sale after we'd sold 25 for the day. I would make 35–40 sales a day and was consistently in the top sales-people for the day. I loved it because I truly believed in what I was selling. But Daniel annoyed the living shit out of me.

He would wear this checked top and have his mousy blond hair gelled back like it was wet. He always had a pen in his pocket but I never saw him use it, not even to get some chicken out of his teeth after eating his chicken and broccoli for lunch every day, because he was getting 'ripped', as he would put it. He smelled like expensive cologne and would pride himself on his motivational talks to the team every morning that consisted of him telling us how good he was and how much he'd spent on the weekend.

We would all retreat to our desks, about as motivated as a sedated bull at a mating factory and start our day. Daniel's desk was positioned at the front of the room, looking out at us like he was the teacher at school. He would put his two feet on the desk, throwing a ball above his head and catching it again. When one of us made a sale, he would yell out to us, 'Well done, darl,' or, 'Good on you, mate, keep going,' because he couldn't be bothered learning our names. Sometimes when I was in the middle of a call, he would sit on the desk beside me. The waft of his man perfume would consume my nostrils, and although it was a gorgeous scent, I have only been able to link the smell with incompetence and frustration ever since.

Daniel would listen to my sales spiel and when his boss joined us for meetings, he would deliver my techniques as his own. I have no doubt he would then use the recordings of my calls to show that his techniques were being applied, so the general vibe towards him from management was, 'How good is Daniel? You'll learn a lot off him.'

Look, there's no doubt about it, Daniel was a fuckstick. I'm sure there's been a time when you have had to deal with someone like this in your workplace or life.

One morning I was catching the tram to work and went to buy a ticket and didn't have the $3 it cost for my ride. I thought I'd risk it, and of course the inspectors came around, asked for my ticket and I copped a $200 fine. During the same trip I received an email telling me that my phone was going to be disconnected unless paid by the agreed extension date, which was that day. In that moment, the anxiety of my other debts slapped me in the face, like the repayments on my car (which I didn't even have anymore, because I'd crashed it into a fence by leaving the handbrake off and only had third party insurance), which were two months behind. My life was a mess and I was trying to stay on top of it.

I slunk into work 25 minutes late. Daniel looked up and smiled, overjoyed that he could assert some authority. He yelled from the other side of the room, 'Good to see you could make it, darl.' *Shut the fuck up, Daniel. Don't lecture me, you incompetent little weasel! You don't even know my name; I'm your top sales rep and you don't know what you're doing!* 'Sorry for being late. It won't happen again,' I yelled out as I got to my desk and affixed my phone headset.

I saw him bounding over with his stupid slicked-back hair and his shitty pen in his pocket that, if sold, could be advertised as 'Never used. Only worn to look important.' The soles of my feet started to burn with anger, as I knew a lecture about being on time was about to tsunami out of his talkhole.

He sat on the desk next to me and exhaled . . . you know, one of those exhales that says, *This is going to hurt me more than it's going to hurt you*, which is a load of crap by the way. It always hurts the person it's being told too far more. He started the conversation with 'Darl . . . what time is it?'

Ahhhhhhhhhh! Internally I was screaming. *You know what time it is, you patronising little snot rag! You've got an expensive watch that you love to flop around like it's an elephant's trunk, showing everyone how well you do in life! So why don't you read it, you arrogant little fucker?* But all I replied was, '9.25,' looking up at him.

He looked down at me in my chair from his power position sitting on my desk. 'And what time do you start?'

WTF! Of course you know what time I start. If you don't know, then you are worse than I thought. You ego-tripping little worm! 'Nine o'clock,' I nervously giggled. 'I'm sorry, it was just one of those mornings and it's the first time I've been late. I'll make sure it never happens again.' I was in a psychological war, and it was easier to just wave my white surrender flag and bow down to the mighty Daniel. Oh, glory the leader and stroke thy ego. Thy shall never tell Daniel to fuck off to thy face.

His eyes sparked with power and he smiled at me. He leant into my face and put his hand on my shoulder. The smell of gingivitis and coffee was like a storm cloud rapidly escaping from his face, penetrating my smelling holes. His eyes were now three inches away from mine. 'You're lucky I'm a nice guy. You don't want to see cranky Daniel. So do me a favour and make sure it doesn't happen again . . . put 9.30 on your timesheet, darl.' He stood up and returned to his desk to meet his quota of ball catches for the day.

I reflected on the conversation and his self-appointed title of 'nice guy'. Okay, first of all, nice guys never call themselves nice guys. Annoying guys call themselves nice guys. Bad guys call themselves nice guys. Do you think when Mother Teresa was thanked for looking after disabled, homeless and hungry people, she would put her hands up in the air and reply with, 'What can I say? I'm a nice lady.' Or when Princess Diana was walking around landmine-affected areas and the media would say, 'Why do you do this, Diana?' Do you think she would put her hands on her hips and reply, 'Well thanks for asking, BBC. I travel around the globe trying to save lives because you know . . . I'm a nice kinda gal! Interview's over, hashtag good deed of the day hashtag nice gal hashtag selfless'?

NO!

Do you know anyone like Daniel? Someone you believe has fluked their way to where they are now? Maybe a colleague was promoted instead of you. Maybe it is your current boss. Maybe it's someone you know who just seems to get lucky breaks all the time. It's very valid that you are frustrated by these types of people.

That afternoon I sat back and observed Daniel. Despite my frustration with him, he was earning $150K a year and I was lucky to pull in $780 after tax a week. So what was he doing that I wasn't? I realised very quickly.

Your job isn't always about being the most skilled

or efficient person in your team. It's also about reading management and seeing what they respond to. What emotion does a boss want to feel when you leave a room after a meeting? You can find the answer to this by observing the people who the boss has promoted or given obvious preference to in the office. What relationship do they have with him/her? Does your boss like to be friends with the people they surround themselves with in management, therefore gaining a reputation of only promoting their friends? Do they need to have not only the professional but the social connection to trust those people with tasks that will advance their career?

So instead of telling yourself, *I don't know what my boss wants from me*, look at the relationship they have with senior staff members around you. It's that easy to see how they like to work and strive to develop that kind of relationship. Don't EVER tell your boss in a meeting, 'I want our relationship to be like . . .' because any effort you make towards that will look contrived. Naturally assert yourself to be seen in that light and watch your relationship bloom.

In this particular case, Daniel was actually a genius. He had identified that his boss liked to look after his mates and needed a social connection with his senior staff. That most deals and professional recruitment decisions were made with a beer in his hand at a bar, and that he loved a punt. So Daniel gave him what he wanted.

One of the team members who started working in the business at the same time as Daniel, and who now worked *for* Daniel, described Daniel as a genius networker. He would invite the boss to the corporate box at the horse-races, pretending he had friends who got free tickets. If the boss accepted, Daniel would quickly go out and buy the best tickets he could find. This gave Daniel a personal connection to the boss that rolled into social drinks, which turned into big nights out, which turned into mutual memories and in-jokes that only they shared compared to the rest of the office. It also gave him many chances to promote himself and define his worth to the company. So all of a sudden Daniel was an average performer who had been identified as having a flair for management. Why? Because he'd told his boss he did, so many times in such subtle ways, that the boss eventually thought it was his own idea.

So Daniel wasn't actually useless. He was just skilled in a different area. He did what he needed to do to get by, and he would do that at all costs. If new management came in, he might have had to start again, but he'd always do better than most of us.

Frustration extinguishes our ability to learn and be open-minded. You have a choice to either be angry and feel robbed by the Daniels of the world, or learn from them. If I had kept my mindset fixed on my anger for Daniel, I would have missed out on learning one of the most critical professional life lessons: there's no such thing as being lucky when it comes to success, people just use different methods to get there. If someone is succeeding without being great at the skills of the primary job they are doing, they must be a genius at doing something else. Whether you perceive that as fair is up to you, but they are there and you aren't, so what can you do to be there next time?

Opportunities for observational learning are all around us. You may have a colleague you perceive as not being very good, but they are at the same level as you. So read their play on how they got there. What do they do that you don't that allows them to have a lower quality of work yet get paid the same?

I bet you are great at your job! So, what if you both read the play and applied your skill? It's a double combo that's rarely used, because reading the play is normally only harnessed by people needing to compensate for their lack of skillset. Put yourself in the power seat by having both.

Don't get me wrong, don't lose your identity or become someone you aren't! If you're a vegetarian and you find out the boss likes steak, don't start going for lunch and devouring T-bones like Fred Flintstone. Or if you don't drink, don't get hammered and vomit in a pot plant at your local RSL. I mean take proactive steps to develop a winning relationship by observing those who are successful around the decision-maker.

I'm not saying book a corporate box, but if you know your boss is interested in Supercars and a big race is on, why don't you ask about it? Google it: you may read that Ford is trying out a new motor technology, and ask your boss if they think it will make a difference. Make sure you research it enough to know the answers, so you aren't a one-sentence wonder. If the boss's team wins, give a high five or reference something from the race.

This isn't selling your soul, it's being socially intelligent. By reading the boss's play, you will have a positive emotion associated with your employment, and that's half the battle.

People love talking about their interests. Tap into what your boss loves, and they will enjoy their conversation with you. When was the last time management socially enjoyed a conversation with you? What are the two primal emotions that people remember? Love and hate, so tapping into love is an easy win.

Because whether we like it or not, we are going to be surrounded by emotion-sucking vampires in the workplace at one time or another. And we cannot run and hide every time someone does not align with us emotionally. We can quit friendships and relationships, so we never have to see people again. But unless we win the lottery or a rich aunty dies, we have to stay in our workplace until we figure out our next move. If you quit a job that you love or need, and your next move is detrimental to your long-term progress, then the arsehole wins. It also means you don't develop the skill set to mentally block out these people. You're letting a negative force rob you at gunpoint of your emotional energy.

You have the superpower to play the game, I know you do! The hardest part is to come home and not spend all your emotional coins reliving the traumatic moments of your day surrounded by pricks. But once you've mastered that, there'll be no stopping you.

GO FOR
CONFIDENCE
NOT EGO

*E*go is perceived in the Western world as being an excess of confidence. Yet ego actually comes from a place of insecurity. I'm sure you're an amazing person, but we all have ego; it just affects us to varying degrees.

An ego can be the engrained title you've given yourself as, for example, 'the breadwinner' of the family. It automatically gives you the superior feeling that you are more valuable than your partner. Or it may make you think that your partner is lucky to have you, and they'll never find someone like you again. Chances are that's true, because you're freaking awesome, but if you genuinely believe that you are better than someone else, that's your ego talking. Confidence, by contrast, is having the emotional intelligence to know you are doing a great job without needing to compare yourself to another person to solidify that knowledge. It's expressed as a deep appreciation for yourself and the people around you.

If you can switch your thinking from ego to confidence, you will become less frustrated, less reliant on other people and external situations to confirm your worth, and more flexible and open to creating a better life for yourself.

Ego can also really fuck you up if it's not being fed. Maybe you are not earning as much money as your partner and that makes you feel inferior. Rather than functioning through your confidence, knowing that money isn't the measuring stick of your self-worth, you might feel indebted to or resentful of your partner. Why? Because your ego doesn't like the way it feels to have someone making more money than you. As a result your relationship probably suffers, you are generally unhappy and the ripple effect takes a toll on your life as a whole.

We live in a time where, in many households, both partners need to work to pay for the lifestyle they want, which can blur the traditional roles of men and women that our parents passed down to us. If you're a mother, you might feel guilty for working while someone else looks after your children, because this dents your 'perfect mum' ego. However, if you stay home with your children, your ego is dented because you feel like you aren't contributing financially to the household, which lowers your worth. Sometimes the ego of your partner reminds you that you're not working for money and forgets that the fucking washing doesn't do itself. Chances are they have been riding their breadwinner ego horse and think that they are failing as a parent by working so much. Or, perhaps you are working and your partner is staying home, or earns less money than you, in which case you too have probably flirted with the thought that you are the only one 'bringing home the bacon'. In these moments, you need to be vulnerable and honest about the way your ego makes you feel. Talk to your partner about it rationally, seeking to find a solution rather than win an argument.

Confidence means knowing that everyone has value. You don't need to be better than someone else to function. You don't need to be a hero or save the day to feel worthy. You just need the confidence to be you.

If you are a single parent and your ex is a dropkick loser, that's cool, you've got this! But letting your ego think that you are better than your ex means you are driving yourself through a negative emotion. You are still pegging your own value against your ex. Be confident that you are doing a great job and release your ego. You are good enough as you are, so don't sell yourself short by needing to tell your ego that you're doing a better job than your ex is. With confidence comes the satisfaction that you did this; you created this life and you deserve it.

Life isn't measured or scored, so why are you competing against other people?

In a business sense, New Age bosses want employees with confidence not ego. If you are leading a team in a certain direction, and it becomes clear that this direction is no longer valuable for the business, ego will not allow you to change it, because to change direction is to admit failure. Ego will put its self-preservation before the business's interests and continue leading a failed strategy, so it can cling to the message that ego is never wrong. But changing direction to seek a more successful path is actually a sign of brilliant confidence, whether that be in a personal or professional sense. You are identifying where you can improve your life or business and confidently changing your path to achieve positive results, despite the damage your ego might suffer in the process.

If ego is believing that you're invaluable, confidence is knowing that you are valuable. Ego needs praise to thrive, while confidence needs only YOU, its vehicle, to thrive. Ego is extreme highs and lows; confidence is a steady path of fulfilment. When ego isn't happy with its performance, it will blame others. When confidence isn't happy with its performance, it will be flexible and look for ways to improve.

In a workplace, confidence isn't fazed by the highs and lows of the egos around them. Confidence can get a hell of a lot of work done while ego is distracted by praise and frustration.

Outside of work, ego is an arsehole, willing to leave you at any moment, making you feel like shit and judging others. Confidence is your best mate, who is by your side through thick and thin. Ego can't find sustainable happiness and has barely any emotional energy for friends/family/hobbies/life. Confidence only needs itself to be satisfied, so it has plenty of emotional energy for family/friends/hobbies/life.

You might have a little ego or you might have a lot. The most important thing is to understand what's driving you in a particular moment: is it ego or confidence?

Being aware of the difference between the two will help you in everyday life. Highly ego-driven personalities are generally intimidating and uncompromising. When we lack confidence, it is hard to debate an ego-driven person. Their ego is so firmly engrained in their psyche, it won't allow them to lose. Because ego-driven people lack confidence, they aren't seeking answers or a new perspective from the debate; they're seeking validation in the immediate win and dominance over a situation. If the other debater is also a highly ego-driven personality, that's when you see debates or arguments get ugly. You have two bulls battling each other that refuse to lose, which means no one wins and no solutions are found.

Being dominated by an egocentric personality can make you mediocre. We tend to settle for what the egocentric personality wants to do, both in relationships and in professional settings, because it's easier than constantly going up against them. When we communicate with such people, we also tend to dumb ourselves down or lessen our contribution (in professional settings) to accommodate the ego's behaviour. But that's not healthy either. We need to work towards being confidently adaptable.

Let's look at an example, shall we? Meet Geoffrey. Geoffrey owns and manages a telecommunications shop. He trains his staff to sell NBN plans because he believes that's the way of the future; he speaks to his staff and tells them how good this would be for the business. Three weeks into this new strategy, Geoffrey realises NBN isn't selling as well as it should be and mobile broadband plans are very popular right now. What does Geoffrey do?

If Geoffrey has based his existence on ego, Geoffrey will find it hard to accept and admit that his strategy was wrong. Rather than putting the business and his staff's commissions first, Geoffrey will keep everyone selling NBN packages because to do otherwise would hurt Geoffrey's ego, which is more important to him than the business.

Or . . .

Confidently adaptable Geoffrey accepts that his original idea to sell NBN wasn't as successful as he had forecast. However, he has identified a different way for the business to make money. Confident in his own ability to adapt the team and point them in the right direction, he changes his plan, to the benefit of his staff and the business.

Being confidently adaptable allows you to pivot and make decisions that are the best for a task and have the best chance of a positive outcome.

Naturally, excessively ego-fuelled personalities hold positions of power within social and professional situations. They may not necessarily be your superior by title, but they will assume themselves superior to your value. This isn't an authentic assumption; this is an assumption for the ego's survival. Think of it as being like ego food. A confident person doesn't need to point out your flaws or perceived flaws; they will understand and support you in a non-intimidating environment that is authentically designed for growth. An ego-based personality, however, will point out your flaws for their own benefit. This might be because they need to tell themselves that they know more than you, or they might gain something by making you act in a certain way. Don't completely dismiss an egocentric personality, though, as they may still have some nuggets of wisdom that help you grow. Remember, you are a confident, flexible and accepting person!

However, sometimes it might be your own ego that gets in the way of accepting advice that might progress you, whether professionally or personally. You might think you're better than the egocentric person advising you and mistake that for confidence, thereby harming your chances of actually feeling confident. If you don't like what you hear from them, ask yourself, *Am I feeling this way because my ego isn't allowing me to progress? Or am I feeling this way because the other person is feeding their own ego and needing to feel dominance over me?* That's something only you can work out in any given situation, but after reading this chapter, you'll have some tools to help you.

As soon as you can identify ego, it will be the moment you stop letting ego control you.

Ego is such a little fucker, though. Sometimes it will camouflage itself as confidence, stifling your growth if you don't recognise its true nature. Say you think you are nailing your confidence levels, when your partner says that you haven't been giving them enough attention lately. This might be a valid comment from someone who loves you. But you are confident that you have been giving your partner lots of attention, so you decide your partner's opinion must be wrong. With confidence, however, comes the wisdom to understand the perspectives of those around you. It's an ego response to dismiss the opinions of others and assume yours is the most important. Therefore, by dismissing your partner's comment without understanding it, you're practising the traits of the ego.

It's important to not only understand ego vs confidence within ourselves, but also when observing and understanding the behaviours of those around us.

If you are the victim of an excessively ego-driven person, quit the emotion of how they are trying to make you feel (go back and read chapter 1 again) and see their behaviour as a communication technique used by someone who isn't feeling great about themselves. Generally, ego is so desperate for validation, those driven by it will manipulate any situation to get it, including starting an argument just to win it. They might bring up a situation from months ago and all of a sudden want to engage in a debate about it. They may navigate a conversation to a place where they know the two of you have disagreed in the past. In this moment there is nothing you can actively do to deflate the emotions of the ego addict. Keep your answers short, don't engage in active debate and inform said egomaniac that you will need to speak about this later. If you identify that the debate is trivial, a simple 'no worries' or 'got it' is a great way to head it off. If you feel yourself rising to the bait, ask yourself, Does YOUR ego need to actively engage in this conversation? Does YOUR ego need to win this trivial debate?

You can think of confidence and ego as being like a sailboat. Confidence is the base of the boat, smoothly sailing across the ocean, creating a solid foundation while keeping its eyes open (if boat bases had eyes) for any change of direction needed to keep everything on board stable. Ego is the erratic flap of the sail in the wind, making all the noise, demanding the attention, insisting that the flap does all the work. The flap thinks it's the only thing that matters on the boat. It is the first thing people see when boat watching, so it has tricked itself into thinking it has the highest value.

But the base of the boat sees the value in everything. It knows that without the base, the sail has nothing to flap from; it knows that without the hull, the workers that look after the base and the sail and everything else would have no shelter. It knows the importance of the boat makers and the trucks that brought the boat to the ramp, understanding that nothing in life has been achieved on the shoulders of just one person (or boat base). The confident boat base also understands the naivety of that ego sail, knowing that the sail might look good and perform well, but its ego will prevent it from fulfilling its potential.

Yet even with that knowledge, the confident boat base accepts the sail for who it is. It knows that the sail, while being incapable of change at this point in time, still plays a vital role in keeping the boat moving, and it appreciates the sail for that. The base of the boat is aware that the fuel for the sail's ego is probably a lack of self-confidence, and when questioned about its performance, the sail gets triggered into a self-preserving anger.

The confident boat base knows how to get the best out of the sail by managing these characteristics. The base of the boat doesn't feel superior to anything and understands everything's value. From the people who made the hammers that helped build the boat, to the people who cleaned the factory of the people who made the hammers that helped build the boat, so many people and things have played vital roles in achieving this present moment. Therefore, the sail's perception that it is the most important member of the team is an obvious sign that it is, in fact, one of the weakest. However, the confident boat base can make peace with this, valuing the sail for what it does and remaining unfazed by the sail thinking it is better than the base. Because the base doesn't have an ego-driven need to think it is superior, the base doesn't lose its shit when its ego isn't fed. And everyone sails smoothly.

You're probably thinking, *I don't need compliments, so I'm fine!* Ego is such a freaking dirty word, commonly associated with divas like Mariah Carey or power-hungry billionaires. However, we have all experienced hurt as a direct result of our ego and we probably always will. The key is to identify it so that when it pops up, we do not take the hurt seriously. We realise it's a fictitious, ego-driven feeling that shouldn't be entertained.

✶

In my twenties I started a fling with a guy called Jason. He was a short, hairy man who was nice enough but he was pretty uptight and *extremely* neat and tidy while I am a messy, disgusting slob of a person and I'm confident within myself about that (*breathe, Jess, use active levels of being confident with who you are, breathe,* as I rock back and forward in the fetal position . . . humming). Jason would get frustrated at me for leaving the toothpaste lid off the tube, so he would escort me to the bathroom like a parent and show me how to screw it back on. Which is fine, it was one of Jason's character traits that showed we were not destined to be together forever, but nobody else wanted to shag us at the time, so it was convenient.

Jason had bought a block of land the year before, but when driving to the plot after work he noticed the sun was in his eyes. Realising the excruciating agony of living a life where the sun would be in his eyes during his ten-minute commute every afternoon, he furiously sold the block of land for a $30,000 loss. Being with Jason was fun when we were shagging, but being around each other before and after that was like the devil's sun in our eyes on the way home. It took us to our intended destination, but the drive was torturous.

So after three months of me driving Jason mad with my messiness, and him driving me mad with his over-the-top judgements about life ('If you don't have your undies colour-coded, are you even living, bro?'), I was sitting in my lounge room one day, by myself in the share house where I lived with three other fabulous piss wrecks. I was broke, hungover from fake Midori, because we couldn't afford the real thing, and eating a microwave lasagne in my undies and oversized Mossimo T-shirt I'd won from collecting Coke labels years earlier.

My Facebook messages popped up and it was Jason. *Hey girl, hope you're having a great day, what you up to,* it said.

I assumed he was alluding to an afternoon rendez-vous, which I had no intention of attending because I hadn't shaved my legs and he drove me nuts. I would have preferred to masturbate with a butcher's knife than go over there that day, too hungover to be lectured about organisation. *Hey not much, just eating microwave lasagne, just spilled some on the floor and didn't clean it up lol, thought you'd like to know,* I replied, assuming I was being sexy and charming.

I've been thinking about us all weekend and I really want us to get together and talk, he replied.

I rolled my eyes because we were at the point of our arrangement where we had to get serious or part ways. I looked down at my hairy legs and my 90 kilo hungover gut that had splashes of spilled lasagne on it (when the gut gets to a certain size, it acts as a catching agent for all food that has fallen victim to gravity). I just hoped I could let him down gently without meeting up with him.

I would have preferred to forcefully drive bamboo up my fingernails than be lectured again on the importance of superannuation.

During this time of pondering, he wrote, *??*, impatiently awaiting a reply.

Oh hey you, been thinking about us all weekend huh? You are falling for me? I replied, while thinking, *Oh god oh god oh god! What a shithouse response. This implies that I too want a relationship and gives him an easy in! Our lives will be ruined if we are together; we can't be together.*

DING!

I looked at my computer and saw his little head pop up in the corner. Nervously I opened the message, preparing myself for the long heartfelt message of love and adoration.

Well, this is awkward, it's actually the opposite. I've met someone and didn't tell them about you. Let's just stop seeing each other altogether, not even as friends. Let's just call it quits. I'm so sorry to send this to you in a message. I wanted to tell you face to face. Thanks so much for everything, it was fun.

My mouth dropped. Was he serious? He was dumping me and not even offering friendship? What the fucking fuck! My stomach turned and I felt hurt, rejected and empty. The fucking nerve of this guy. I was going to dump him, not the other way around! What was wrong with me that I wasn't good enough for this hairy little sun-hating fuckstick? I blocked him immediately without replying, called my housemates and told them to bring another bottle of fake Midori home.

The feeling of being empty and worthless swamped my inner ego like a tsunami. I drowned in the ego hurt. The rest of my evening was plagued with fake Midori shots with my housemates, a boob tube dress and a dance floor at 3 am, where I was yelling at a guy with a mohawk that all guys are cunts.

But let's break it down. Jason's actions had inflamed my inner prick's fear of not being loved (a separate issue that generally rides side by side with ego). My ego of needing to be the centre of his world fuelled this situation. Yet I'd been going to quit him anyway, so he had just done the hard work for me. Plus, he had found someone he genuinely liked and who liked him, so they had potentially found happiness with each other and were starting an exciting adventure. In order for my ego to survive in this situation, I would have preferred to break his heart, to wish him pain, while achieving the same outcome. With his pain would come my ego's comfort. How is that a fair and fulfilled way to live your life? Yet ego twists our minds to seek the demise of those around us, in order for us to successfully grow and live. It's like a weed in our subconscious thoughts, not allowing anyone to thrive or be happy, including ourselves.

Your ego manipulates you and allows others to as well. If you are not confident in an area of your life, and you rely on someone or something to feed your ego to feel successful, your ego is manipulating you to play the role of someone's puppet. You're no longer playing your authentic game, but the game you think someone else wants you to play. If you've ever said, 'I'm just a shit magnet for men/business partners/*insert anyone else in your life here*', it's because you're feeding the ego of a need in your life, as opposed to being confident in who you are and making the right choices for you.

You might tell yourself that you are a brilliant business person or you're wanting to be one, so when you look for business partners, you won't want to hear the hard truths about how your business can grow. That's too hard on the ego. So naturally you go for the person who tells you what you want to hear, and you leave the meeting feeling great because your ego bucket is full. You hire that person because of the way they made you feel and not because they are the best choice for your business. That's ego.

You might meet a guy, and he tells you how beautiful you are. After a few weeks he turns into a fucking loser and starts sleeping at your house, because he got evicted from his unit for a reason that was obviously completely someone else's fault. But your ego needs to feel like you are loved, and he has ticked that box. So ego allows your irrational view of this situation, and the fear of being alone overrides your confidence that you will find someone else, making you stay with him. The thing is, our ego compensates for what we feel the most insecure about. Ego has no stability, so when the comfort of ego is taken away from us, we start to act like irrational dickwads.

Stop manipulating yourself into relying on someone to make you feel worthy. Kill your ego and allow yourself to become completely vulnerable about who you are. Build the base of your confidence on that vulnerability. Be your authentic self, because how can you have confidence in a character you've created, based on what you think everyone else wants you to be?

4

BUILD THE FOUNDATION OF YOUR BEING

According to the internet gods, the Dalai Lama, when asked what surprised him most about humanity, said:

Man.

Because he sacrifices his health in order to make money.

Then he sacrifices money to recuperate his health.

And then he is so anxious about the future that he does not enjoy the present;

the result being that he does not live in the present or the future;

he lives as if he is never going to die, and then dies having never really lived.

✷

We all need a solid foundation for our being, values that keep our souls alive and keep us from merely existing as opposed to really living. Merely existing is an easy trap to fall into. We all look for different ways to bring us comfort and feel like we are worth something.

As I said in chapter 2, when mapping out the origin of my inner prick, in my early twenties, I tried to find salvation in the magical penis, as many young people do. I thought having a boyfriend and being loved was all I needed to survive in life. Yet the more I wanted it, the more I forced the idea of simply wanting to be loved, as opposed to finding the right person who I could love and would love me too. It took me a while to realise that giving a blow job to a guy in his car outside the club was not a shortcut to fulfilment. If it was, Buddhist temples would be lined with hundreds of dark blue 1998 Holden Commodore Calais, letting us jump in and give the spiritual penis a gobby, feel enlightened, adopt an orphan and all live happily ever after. But unfortunately, NO! Bummer, right?

So what the fuck do we base the foundation of our being on? It's a deep, deep question.

The foundation of your being needs to be solid. It's like building a pizza oven. If you build it on a shit piece of wood, it will eventually crumble and fall down. You need emotional bricks that you can rely on. The only thing you can control in your life is yourself, your own state of mind. So that's probably your only choice for the foundation . . . sorry about that. Everything else is secondary.

This includes your kids. It's not fair on them to build your foundation on their existence. YES, for us parents, they're a huge part of our lives, and we love them and they rule our world. But unless you want to be that mum or dad who hates your kid's girlfriend or boyfriend, thinking nobody is ever good enough for them and ending up driving them away or creating a toxic environment, you cannot base your entire life's meaning around your kids. That's a shortcut, short-term solution that will end up in you being lost and angry when they move out.

Your kids also aren't here to right your wrongs. They are not your redemption story. They aren't here to learn from your mistakes, so you can feel comfort in them not doing what you did, they are here to learn from making their own mistakes. You can't build the foundation of your being on the hope your kids will turn out better than you. It's not in your control, so you will be destined to suffer if you try it. Yes, give them advice, but you don't give them orders. (Unless it's about meth or guns or petrol bombs, you know, the obvious stuff.)

Other transient stuff that you shouldn't build your foundation on includes work! Yes, it's cool to live for your work. But what are you going to do if it's all taken away from you tomorrow?

When you let go of the control that's required to make something your entire foundation, you don't need it as much. And when you don't need it, you can enjoy it more. You can live more in the present. You will probably find your relationships with your children will improve; your work will improve. Because you do not have the pressure of something transient being the base of your life. You'll still work hard and have goals; the object of this is not to quit the job that you love. It just means that you can create a strong foundation in your mind and build the love of your job on top of that. Then, for example, when something goes bad at work, your entire life won't fall apart, which will allow you to fix the problem rather than be overwhelmed by stress.

Everything you need to build your foundation is in your mind. You can side salad it with any values and goals you might have, but it is the love and fulfilment you have inside you that will allow you to be anywhere in the world, feeling the same way. Nobody nails this all the time, by the way. I'm sure even the Dalai Lama has been in a bad mood once or twice in his life. However, the challenge is to create a sustainable positive mindset and narrative about yourself that stops you from relying on external events to validate a rocky foundation.

Once you've built this internal foundation, you won't even need your partner. This means you can choose to be with them and enjoy them more, because you aren't relying on them to give your life meaning. What a weight off everyone's shoulders! It might sound selfish at first, but it's not. What's actually selfish is relying on your relationships as a shortcut to validation, or relying on a career to define your identity.

Everything in your life will improve if you stop NEEDING it and start ENJOYING it. Work because you love it, not because of how much money it's going to give you. Your decision-making will improve because your goal becomes the quality of work and not the financial gain, which gives your mind more room for improvement. Love your partner, your kids, your friends because you love them, not because you need them.

The Dalai Lama has also said, 'The goal is not to be better than the other man, but your previous self.' Good on ya, DL – our journey is like nobody else's. So why the freaking shit are we comparing ourselves to others? By comparing, we are still validating our foundation through the external observations of other people. The true key of internal thinking is to feel no negative emotions about the accomplishments of other people, even if you don't like them. This is YOUR foundation; you are the builder.

✗

There's one shitty foundation-building material that we all use: MONEY! It's the most transient material of them all, yet we all say we'll be happy once we buy a house/ get a good savings plan/earn enough money to retire early. Even Paris Hilton has said once she earns a billion dollars, she'll be happy. But when we get to your financial goal, and once the buzz of accomplishment dies down, we find it's a one-way road to feeling as empty as when we started. So we assume we need more money and more things to fulfil us. We waste our lives chasing a rabbit we'll never catch, feeding ourselves the delusion that a number in our online bank account will solve all of our internal problems. We mistake the excitement of nice things with validation and happiness. We start to need these things to feel worthwhile. By building your internal worth, you can still have nice things, but you can enjoy them far more. You will not align these things with the reason for your existence, so you'll be free to make them objects of pure joy.

We have a perception if we make a certain amount of money, it will bring us happiness. I wrote this while on one of the Gili Islands, Meno (not the busy one). Meno had been devastated by an earthquake eighteen months earlier. As I walked around, I came across the rubble of a local house that used to stand on the beachfront. It was clear that it would have been a place of prestige. I could still see the beautiful timber workmanship on the doors, the birds and fish and flowers that would have been carved with such pride. A swing was still attached to a fallen tree, the garden overgrown with weeds, the concrete stairway nothing but rocks and dust. The house itself had a thatched roof that was now on the ground, with the frames of the house caved in like it was a matchstick school project that didn't have enough glue. There was an eerie silence that I hadn't expected to find anywhere in Bali, especially such a tropical paradise.

You assume that somewhere so beautiful is always going to have its damaged homes rebuilt, but maybe this island had been forgotten? Outside the house ruins was a young woman, long hair in a bun, wearing a pair of black tights and an old ripped green T-shirt with an eight-month-old boy in a green sling on her front. She looked at me and asked, 'Do you want coconut oil?' I replied with, 'No, thank you,' and she said, 'No problem,' and continued to sweep the cracked pavement with her grass broom. But it wasn't a normal sweep; it was a slow sweep that looked like the broom weighed 100 kilos, as if moving it was physically painful for her. She walked around for a few seconds, swept and then swept again in the same time frame. Sometimes sweeping the pavement that she'd swept before, achieving nothing new.

There was an air of sadness about her. When she kissed her son, after every few sweeps, he would look up at her with gorgeous brown eyes through long eyelashes and give her a smile. When she looked back at him,

I could see that the child was giving her peace, her dry lips forming a half-smile that seemed to break the long drought of sadness that was plaguing her. But when the baby looked away, her sadness would return.

She wandered another few steps and swept. I wondered why the path was so clean yet the house had been in ruins for over eighteen months and I would suspect looked exactly the same as it did the day of the earthquake.

Our eyes met, and my social anxiety said, *Stop looking at this woman. She'll think you want to rob her or take her coconut oil or . . . okay, just stop looking.* But I couldn't. What did she need to ease this sadness? We have an expectation that money will make everyone happy in poor countries. If I want to help someone, I assume the question is, 'How much money do you need?' That will solve everything!

As I continued to stare at her, she looked a little startled, like she had misinterpreted a request I had made. She asked again, 'Sorry, do you want coconut oil? Can I help you?'

I smiled at her and asked, 'What is your son's name?' I pointed at him with the warm smile on my face that is universal code for *I'm a mother as well.*

'Ari,' she replied with a smile, as Ari looked at me and handed me a small pearl-coloured shell that he'd been playing with.

I said, '*Nama saya* Jessie.' Which is, 'My name is

Jessie,' and the only Indonesian I remember from my year 9 Indonesian classes. I wished I hadn't wagged so many classes to buy hot chips and a chocolate milk; I could have really used the local lingo at this point.

She smiled and said, 'Ahhhhhh, hello.' We stood awkwardly for a few seconds, then giggled at the same time, which in my mind was polite sounds for, *What the fuck do you want? I have an entire path to sweep and am carrying a child, so hurry it up, toots.* We stood awkwardly again in silence, the only sound the clucking of a nearby chook.

She pivoted to turn away from me, bookending our conversation with another large sweep. Before her back was completely turned, I asked her with a sped-up high-pitched tone, 'Are you okay?' Her eyes told me she hadn't understood this chipmunked nervous voice, so I tried again. 'Are you okay? You look sad. Is this your house?'

Her eyes filled with tears and she looked down at her son. 'Mother's house.' She stroked her son's back, turned her back and started to sweep again. She obviously didn't want to talk about it, and I didn't want to be that tourist who asks traumatised locals about the devastation in their country to gain 'cultural knowledge' that could be readily found online.

As she walked away, I couldn't help making one final plea. 'Can I help?' I yelled out to her. 'Can I help you sweep, or can I give you some money for you and your son?' The sweeping stopped. She turned around and walked back to me at a pace much faster than before. This time her face had changed from sad and lost to determined and cold.

'Thank you,' she started as I reached for my purse. 'No, no, no, no, I don't want money . . . money killed my mother.'

I looked confused and stood silent, as I had expected her to say, 'Yep, give me ya cash, sister.' (It's what I would have said!)

Her eyes moved from cold to tormented as she turned and squinted at the rubble of her home.

'Money ran through my mother's blood; she forgets what makes her happy. She gets taken over with money and thinks that is her god. Every day she thinks about money, every day she tells me we need more money. I ask her, "What for? We have food and we have house and family and health. Why you need more money?" She says it's because "the more money we have, the more happiness we have. Our neighbours will think we are better than them, we can get a better house, everyone will want to be like us." I don't know why she worries about being better. Why do you get energy from showing people you have nice things and others don't? Why does other people's sadness make you have more energy? If you want nice things, that's okay, but you shouldn't want nice things just to show people.

'My sister had a child before the earthquake. My mother didn't come see the baby; she just wanted to make more money for the baby. She thinks if the baby has lots of money it will have a good life. She worshipped money like it was a god that was going to bring us great health and happiness. But my sister is sad and the baby is sad because they want my mother for comfort. That is something she can do for free and costs no money.'

As she was talking, a small spider fell onto her arm and she gently placed it on a tree. She must have seen me take extra interest in her spider relocation techniques, and she shook her head again. 'Many tourists kill the spiders,' as she slapped her arm to show me what we did. 'Why? Just as easy to place it on the tree. Why do you want to kill?'

I told her we worried that the spider was going to hurt us and make us sick.

She smiled and said, 'Small spider doesn't make you sick. When we are scared, humans kill, sometimes each other, sometimes spiders, but we always kill when we are fearful. If you stop being fearful then you will stop killing.'

(That said, while writing this down as I sat at an old restaurant table dumped on the side of a dirt track on Gili Meno, a broken vase next to me filled with old Sprite cans, under a tree that's tangled in rusted fairy lights, overlooking the ocean, I killed a fly because I didn't like the way its furry little legs walked on my skin. Note to self: *be wiser next time . . . be wiser next time . . .* Hang on . . . be right back . . . there's a guy with one tooth missing, smoking a ciggie trying to sell me a sarong.

SHIT, I BOUGHT ONE! I didn't need one! Paid him $35 – the price for three – and he walked away thinking he was the best salesman ever. Started singing the national anthem, blew a smoke ring for me through the gap in his teeth and finished it with 'Aussie, Aussie, Aussie!' What a legend! Anyway.)

The woman said, 'Once people stop being fearful, they'll stop killing. That's what killed my mother,' as she looked straight into my eyes like it was the first time she'd said it out loud. Her eyes widened and a fresh breeze brushed her hair across her face in what seemed like a cleansing motion.

'Did someone kill her?' I asked nervously, as I didn't want to take her to a place of torment again.

'No.' She looked back at me, her eyes latching onto mine as if to say, *This is the most important thing I have to say to you.* 'Money killed my mother. When the earthquake happened there were no tourists. There was no money; we were all the same. We all ate from the ocean and we only had each other. My mother put all of her prayers and her energy into making money again; when she didn't have any, she didn't feel like she was a person anymore. She had her children and her grandchildren, but that wasn't enough. She forgot how to be a person. She only knew her worth by how much money she had. She walked up and down this path every day, trying to sell and make money from everyone on the island, but no one is buying.'

I asked again, 'How did that kill your mother? Did she get sick?'

She stroked her baby. He looked up at her, lengthened his cute little arm and offered her a piece of apple mango that he'd been eating. She looked at him, shook her head indicating that he should eat it and kissed him on the head. While still looking down at him, she replied, 'She killed herself. This is why I don't know why people worship money like a god. Everyone thinks life will be better if they have money, like they think life will be better if they have god. But it is a sickness. My mother got sick many years ago when it took hold of her. It was all she talked about, it's all she cared about. But wealth has no loyalty. It will leave you when there is trouble. People kill each other over it. It makes people want to do bad things like drugs and jealousy.

'I will never understand. Yes, we need money to buy medicine and to have a house, but some people lose their spirits trying to find it. Some people make money and keep their spirits and others lose them. So this is my mother's land and this was her house. But I am giving it to the local people to build a school and hospital. No longer will this land be sick, no longer will this land have my mother's spirit. She can be free.'

My mind flashed to all the times I had been consumed by money as opposed to the journey. I had felt like my life would be better if I had a new car or a new kitchen. These things are good to strive for, but a terrible foundation to rest your soul on.

The self-help books we read say, 'You need to be better . . . You need to work less . . . You need to work more . . . Nine easy steps to making a million dollars in six months.' We finish the book and say to ourselves, *I'm going to do that! I'm going to be a better person because I am going to make a million dollars in six months*. But we never do. There should be millions of people working a four-hour day and living their best lives, but instead we just feel guilty and worthless, because the book told us how to make a million dollars by working four hours a day and we didn't do it.

It's common sense that we need to make an income and provide for ourselves, pay our bills and strive for whatever makes our heart sing. But we cannot base the foundation of our soul on something that is external to us, like money or a car or a kitchen bench. Don't get me wrong, they're nice to have, but we need to look inside ourselves for our foundation.

Build your own internal foundation. Quit the narrative that you are not good enough without a lot of people and material objects around you. Be your own best friend. Turn the external things you've previously based your worth on into a blessing, not a necessity, so you can enjoy them more. If you feel like you have no blessings, build your internal worth and your external blessings will become more apparent. It's a much nicer flow-on effect than having those around you tear down your walls.

ASK FOR WHAT YOU WANT

*T*he creator of *The Block* said to me once, 'Life is a game, why are you so afraid to play it? Be kind, show compassion, but if there's an answer you are seeking, just ask the question to the person who has the answer. And if that person doesn't want to give you the answer, then you can conclude that the answer to your question has been refused. So then you can stop worrying about what will happen if you ask the question, and your quest for closure has been achieved.' Probably the best advice I've ever had while smoking a cigarette on the rear bumper of a VW SUV, waiting for some tilers to arrive.

It sounds simple in theory. But when you combine the internal narrative of our worth with our perception of who we are asking, and the story and emotional baggage we associate with that personality, not to mention being over-sensitive to minor events because we take everything in life too personally, asking the simplest questions to our boss or friends or whoever we seek clarity from is like trying to fold origami with turds for fingers.

I once needed to ask for a reference from a former boss, who I assumed hated me because I assume everyone hates me, especially men of power and age, based off the internal narrative that I learnt as a child. I spent days hypothesising what my former boss would say, assuming that he would tell me no. I reflected on all the times I'd felt let down by him, along with imagining what he would have said about me when I left the business. How negatively narcissistic can you get, assuming EVERYONE is talking about you when you leave a place of business? By any external markers, my time there had gone very smoothly, yet my mind was so addicted to negativity, I felt that I'd been a nightmare of an employee.

My stomach was in knots. If you've ever had to have a tough conversation, you know that sick, anxious feeling, where you would rather sacrifice the quality of your own life than confront something or someone to sort out a situation or ask a question so you can progress in life.

So I left it, for six whole months. In this time I practised the prick cleanse (go back and re-read chapter 6). I also found the source of my inner prick (chapter 2) and realised the narrative I had told myself was something I'd learnt over time from others and not my authentic self. Through this work, my mind created positive neural pathways towards being confident within myself and feeling like I wanted progress, and the only way I was going to get that was to ask a six-word question: 'Can I have a reference, please?'

Your prick cleanse is just not about yourself and other people; it's also about situations. I was close to getting my dream job, and the only thing stopping me from getting it was asking that six-word question . . . six freaking words! My inner narrative had turned into quite the storyteller, and I was believing the creative facts it fed me. Why wouldn't I? My brain is my friend, right? If it tells me, *Your former boss is probably going around celebrating you've left, didn't appreciate you, didn't value you, didn't even like you*, why wouldn't I believe it and use it as real evidence to resent this man and, of course, be anxious to ask for a reference? We've established your brain can't be trusted and we need to train it, just like a dog, to learn how to behave in an honest and proper manner. Because if you don't, your brain practically shits everywhere and fights with all of the other dogs at the park. So, as I cleansed and stripped away the emotion, I realised that most of the hatred I perceived from others was a narrative I told myself. And even if everything was as bad as I had initially thought, I still wanted that dream job, so I needed to ask for that reference. That question could change my life!

When you don't ask for what you want, you're filling a fake pride you have within yourself. Even if you have the lowest confidence, you don't ask because YOU don't want to feel a certain way if they say no. YOU don't want them to think a certain way about you. YOU don't want to inconvenience them. It's all about YOU. But keeping yourself at the centre of the reason why you don't do something is actually fucking you up more than any enemy could. Because YOU will never end up doing what is right for YOU!

So while you think you're doing the right thing, you're just existing in this world, trying to please others and getting angry at yourself or depressed, which ripples out to your personal relationships, devaluing your self-worth even more. You go from participating in the game of life to having someone else move your pieces as your authentic self plummets deeper and deeper into a distant memory. Before you know it, you'll be 60 and you'll have been doing what everyone else wants you to do for your entire life. You'll probably unintentionally take it out on your partner and your children. And as you take it out on them, you'll be screaming on the inside, *I AM NOT THAT PERSON. I USED TO BE A HOOT!* You might be feeling that way now. I know I have in the past, when I was participating in someone else's game and not asking for what I wanted, whether in relationships, friendships or at work.

Let's handle what happens if they say no, or the answer isn't what you had hoped. It shouldn't faze you, because the only thing you should be thinking is how proud you are of yourself for having the confidence to stand up and take control of your life. Mathematically, by adopting the approach of believing you are worth asking a question or having a conversation to progress in life, you will always progress faster than you will be held back.

So I called my former boss and discovered he was happy to hear from me and genuinely interested in what I'd been up to. I had the reference in my inbox within 45 minutes. It had taken me six months to ask, and 45 minutes to receive. What a mathematical brain-fuck! When we have something we want to ask for, we aren't seeking to become contortionists. But the way we twist ourselves up to protect our pride hinders us to the point where it would feel easier to put our ankles behind our ears than ask one sentence.

✱

Here are two more examples of asking for what you want. One was a disaster, but it's part of the exercise and practice of asking. We can't run and hide under the bed every time someone says no to our question. We are playing the game of life here, remember? Every time you land on someone's hotel in Monopoly, do you pack up the pieces and hide under your bed? NO, because it's a game. The same rules apply here; strip away the emotion and stop filling your pride and ego.

Last year I had an idea for a TV show where we help people around the country, but to do the show properly I needed one million dollars. I needed someone to fund it, and Clive Palmer was the richest guy I knew. We had only met each other once for a radio interview, but I still had his number saved in my phone. I still remember sitting on our back verandah, empty XXXX cans littered in front of me from a BBQ the night before, wearing a pair of maternity swimmers because I was blowing out in the guts from a pastry addiction I couldn't beat, and four days of underarm hair growth. *Fuck it, I'm calling, life's a game. But what if Clive laughs at me? Oh whack that, Jess, who cares! Do I value Clive Palmer laughing at me or getting one million dollars to help Australian families?* I called the number and it rang!

'Hello,' he answered.

My heart beat a million miles an hour and my palms went sweaty. I wanted to hang up, but it was just a question. I paused for a moment. 'Hi Clive, I'm Jess and I have an idea that will make you look great, help Australians and I only need one —'

'I'm just getting on a plane. I'll call you back when I land!' he interrupted and hung up.

I couldn't believe it. Clive Palmer was calling me back! I went to the fridge and got a bottle of rosé to celebrate. Could asking for what you want really work? Who would have thought to get an answer you just needed to ask the question! I poured another glass of rosé, then another and another. With each glass, the chances of the funding coming through became higher in my mind. I looked at myself in the reflection of the glass door in front of me. Staring back was 85 kilos of white chocolate, messed-up hair with six months of roots regrowth, a swimming onesie. I raised a cheers to myself, as if I was drinking with my reflection, and thought, *God, you look good.* I was obviously tanked, because if I'd wandered into a forest in that state, I'd have been mistaken for a wild animal and shot. With each glass of celebratory rosé, my perception of reality grew fainter and my mind warped into a delusion that I'd already secured the million dollars from Clive Palmer! I just needed him to return my call to finalise the details, but hey, I didn't know how long he'd be in the air for.

Three hours passed. I was onto my third bottle of rosé, listening to jazz music from the 80s and smoking some leftover fat-stained cigarettes I found under the BBQ. Picture me pelvic thrusting in my maternity one-piece floral bathers, rosé in one hand, ciggie in the other. The more intoxicated I got, and you know what this is like, the more I believed my own bullshit. Sometimes, it's crying on the side of the road screaming, 'I'm all alone and nobody loves me!' In this instance, it was that Clive Palmer was definitely keen to give me a million dollars.

I decided to call Mum and let her know the great news! No need to be weighed down by the finer points like Clive knowing about my proposition, agreeing, transferring money, having a production company, creating a TV show, getting it picked up by TV execs. The unimportant details. She answered, and in a slur I yelled, 'MUM, I JUST SECURED ONE MILLION DOLLARS FOR A TV SHOW!'

'Oh, that's nice!' Mum slurred back.

I realised we were at equal levels of intoxication. 'I've got to go, Clive's probably trying to call. Love you!'

'Love ya, darling, can I tell anyone?' she responded.

'Of cooooooooooooourse!' I screamed. Why wouldn't ya want to celebrate raising a million fake dollars in one night? A distant, logical voice whispered in the background, so softly I could barely hear it, *Jess, all you've done is call Clive. He doesn't know what the idea is, he hasn't called you back, you haven't even written a plan for a TV show, and people don't just hand over one million dollars because some drunk called them at six o'clock at night. DO you think letting everyone know about something that hasn't happened yet is a good idea? What if it doesn't come through?*

*What are you going to tell people? You're jumping the g—*I drowned out that negative voice with another sip of rosé . . . *Shut the fuck up, logical voice! Just let a girl dance by herself to jazz music in a one-piece with some cheap wine and celebrate something that hasn't happened yet.*

My next memory was the sound of a crow and warm sunlight on my face. It was the following morning and I'd fallen asleep on the outdoor lounge. Norm and the kids were inside, and I could hear Norm yelling out to them, 'Don't go outside!' My eyes weren't open yet but I'd clearly been involved in a gunfight overnight and someone had shot me in the temple, or else something far worse had happened.

Oh, it turned out I was just hungover on $4 rosé. I tried to close my mouth but it felt like paper. I tried to swallow but my throat was like the barren rivers in the middle of a drought-ridden western NSW farm. As I breathed out, my face was struck with a scent bomb of ashtray and dogshit. I sat up like I was starring in a safe roads commercial and I'd sustained a spinal injury from not wearing a seatbelt.

Norm was looking lovingly at me through the kitchen window, an odd reaction to a mother of two who had passed out on the outdoor lounge setting. As I sat up, he came out and handed me a coffee, kissing me on the cheek. He glowingly said, 'I'm proud of ya!'

What the fuck is he talking about? 'Thanks,' I replied, gratefully taking the coffee. I wracked my brain to try and decipher my actions from the night before, and why my morning would be filled with praise as opposed to judgement. Maybe I'd woken up in an alternate universe where being unstable and a piss wreck was seen as brave and noble. Where self-doubt was seen as wise and fat was seen as skinny. If that was the case, get my fucking crown now. I am your leader!

Norm sat next to me and looked into my eyes with pure admiration. 'I can't believe Clive Palmer gave you one million dollars last night. I knew you could do it!'

I coughed/choked/squirmed out loud. 'Oh yeahh-hhhh, I forgot about that,' I nervously replied, looking around for my phone. *Where the fuck is my phone!* Before saying anything else, I needed to know if Clive had called back. No need to tell everyone I got carried away after three bottles of rosé and just assumed it was real if he's called back and left a voicemail saying, 'Hey, it's Clive, just touched down. I don't really know you, I don't know what you were calling for, but do you want one million dollars for a TV show?' I knew the chances were low . . . *But where the fuck is my phone!* Norm looked so happy. *Piss wreck, Jess, piss wreck!*

I found my phone: sixteen missed calls, two voice-mails. *Yeeeeeeeeow!* I didn't even look at the number before playing the first voicemail . . . 'Voicemail received at 8.25 pm – Hey, Flange,' Ah shit, it was my friend Jacquie, who calls me Flange. 'Hey, a Thai lady at the restaurant just said I've got the perfect nose and apparently Thai people think it's the perfect shape, how good's livin'? – to delete this voicemail press five.' I pressed five like it was the button to prevent a nuclear reaction. 'Voicemail received at 8.28 pm – Flange, do you think . . .' Five! 'Voicemail deleted.' I checked my missed calls. All sixteen were from Jacquie.

I turned from my phone and looked back at Norm's adoring eyes. 'Well, I think I got a bit ahead of myself. He said he would call me back because he was getting on a plane, and I couldn't explain to him exactly what it was or that I needed one million dollars.'

His admiration turned to laughter and then confusion. 'You made me call my sister and tell her!' he responded, his face scrumpled like he was slightly worried about my mental state. But it was hard to feel immediate emotion for an event I couldn't remember, when my liver felt like it was about to be rejected from my abdomen after being transplanted from a pig. I had to pee the only liquid left in my body, and I had no interest in taking responsibility for my actions.

'Honey, why would you believe anything I say on rosé?' I lay back down on the outside lounge as Norm stood up and walked inside. If I hadn't been dying of unnatural causes, I'd have engaged in a world of anxiety about what his sister thought of me, what he thought of me, my failures as a parent and a partner, but I was too sick to engage. Plus I needed to rebuild my strength for when Clive called. I closed my eyes and fell asleep, phone in armpit to feel the vibrations of my destiny when he finally called back.

I stayed by my phone, not leaving it for a second for the rest of the day, then week . . . then month. It's now been eighteen months since that phone call, so unless he's travelling to Mars, I reckon he's landed. I tried calling him a few more times, but he'd obviously saved my number as 'do not answer'.

HOWEVER! Piss wreck aside, let's strip away the emotion of what happened before the rosé incident. I didn't and still don't care that it didn't pay off, because I asked the question. And by learning to ask the hard questions without attaching emotion to them, you will create more opportunities than you will lose. Embarrassment is an ego-filled emotion that stifles our success. When you ask for something you want in life, you will succeed regardless of the answer you're given, because you have decided your self-worth is your top priority. If you genuinely desire something to happen, you need to ask the question and accompany it with whatever you think is needed to make the answer a yes. So please start exercising this in your everyday life and relationships. I wouldn't be writing this book if I hadn't asked to write one.

I'm currently wearing my ugg boots, no bra, a jumper with a coffee stain that starts at the titties and runs to the gut, and some underarm odour that would kill a cat. My English teacher at school told me I would never get a job that involved writing. I can't really spell, my grammar is as erratic as Charlie Sheen's moods, and when I tell the other mums at school pick-up that I'm writing a book, they look at me and respond in a high-pitched voice, 'Ohhhhhhhh, a kids' book?'

When I had the idea for the book, I asked the management team that had taken us on after *The Block* to set up a meeting with a book publisher. When I told Norm what I had asked for, he looked at me affectionately and braced me for rejection. 'Don't get your hopes up. I hope you get it, but I just don't want you to be deflated.' His eyes creased as he tried to figure out how to protect me from any hurt that would follow such a ridiculous request.

I looked at him and smiled. 'I'll be fine.'

When people try to shield you from pain, most of the time they aren't intentionally trying to stop you from reaching your goals. You're just embarking on a journey that they wouldn't have the courage to do. They feel the journey as if it was happening to them, and their love for you is subconsciously bringing you down to meet their fear. When this happens, don't waste your energy on roaring like a tiger and screaming your fearlessness to a person who has nothing to do with the goal you have set yourself. Obviously, if the person who doesn't believe in you has anything to do with the decision-making process for you to achieve your goal, then pitch your arse off about how amazing you are! But in the case of your partner worrying about you being rejected, show them in results. Your fearlessness will inspire them to become their authentic self, turning away from fear, more than anything you could say beforehand.

I was scheduled to meet the publisher, a woman called Cate, at 11 am at management's office in the city of Sydney. If this was a motivational, fire-walking inspirational DVD set, I would tell you that to prepare I wrote *You are amazing* on my mirror, meditated, took an ice bath, glued together a mood board and saved an orphan from poverty on the morning of my meeting. I then walked into that meeting confident, nailed it, was offered a book deal on the spot and then went out and shot a deer. But, let's be honest, this is real life; we can teach ourselves the tools to be fantastic, but it takes time to build up that swagger. Nobody, not even Tony Robbins, would have figured it all out in 48 hours. And it's a huge shame we don't talk much about the process and failures leading up to emotional freedom and confidence. I'll be honest: I WAS SHITTING BRICKS! I'd never pitched a book before. When Mum used to place our lunch orders at school, she'd spell pizza as PITZA! She said it was the authentic way to spell it, and I would fight viciously with anyone who challenged her in Mr Walker's grade 2 class.

On the morning of the book pitch, my inner prick was telling me how stupid I was for even wasting this lady's time. *You're shit, you're hopeless.* I had to whack all of those narratives that like to spring up and halt anything progressive happening to our lives. Of course something new is scary! If it was familiar to us, we wouldn't be worried, but then we also wouldn't progress in our lives. Every human on the planet, no matter how successful they are, still dreams of doing something more with their lives. Even if that's to landscape the garden or build a pergola, progression is what makes us tick.

I had prepared five pages of gear for the book pitch, which included a half-nude picture of myself with my puppy's face pasted over my areolas and a badly written rant about how we have forgotten to value ourselves, and we are the greatest things to ever happen to us . . . because we are all we have at the end of the day. I was dressed in a white floral top and pale blue jeans and had even bought some heeled boots for $24.99 from Kmart. If sex sells, I was selling out that day. The plan was: finish Sydney breakfast show at 10 am, run out of the office, 25-minute drive to the publisher's office, achieve life goals, go home, pop open a sugar-free Vodka Cruiser, the end.

As the clock approached 10 am, I was packing my notebook and laptop in my bag when the boss approached us. 'Can I see you all for a research meeting?' *FUCK!* I'd forgotten all about research day. *Fuck fuck fuck!* Six of us, the four on-air people, a producer and the boss, then gathered in a small office with a signed AC/DC guitar on the wall and a large computer screen for PowerPoint presentations. For a research meeting, the radio station uses a computer to generate a picture of our typical listener. They crunch data they have collected from listeners to our station, like age, sex, occupations, blah blah, so we can talk about things those people are interested in. Based on 400 people, the computer spits out a picture of a brown-haired, brown-eyed dude who looks about 40 and has excellent dental hygiene. They call him Darren, because it's probably easier to type 'Darren' instead of 'typical listener' 400 times into a PowerPoint presentation. Darren likes to go to the pub with his mates but also values family time. Darren uses power tools yet isn't necessarily a tradie, but he does like to potter around the home and fix things, and sometimes he likes to go see a movie that's probably a comedy. So just talk about things Darren would like, got it?

I looked at my phone and it was 10.35, and the drive to the book pitch was 25 minutes. *Go fuck yourself, Darren, why do you have to have so many hobbies? I need to go!* My internal hatred for Daz and his thousand hobbies was startled by the boss asking, 'Does everyone understand?' The meeting was over so I grabbed my laptop and dashed towards the exit like a drug mule leaving an airport terminal.

Just as my $25 black Kmart boots were about to hit the doorway, our producer, Laura, pulled me aside. 'Jess, can I see you for a second?' That stress vs nausea vs constipation feeling struck my stomach. You know that one, when you're really time poor and shit just keeps happening? I walked back and stood next to her, and her mouth started getting closer to my face. What the hell was happening? It got closer and felt like slow motion; I could see the fine hairs glimmering on the side of her face. Was she having a nervous breakdown or were my $25 boots really impressing the ladies today? Her mouth diverted to the left-hand side of my head and approached my ear. She whispered, 'You've got period all over your jeans.' *FUCKKKKKKKKKKKK!* I screamed in my head. I didn't have time to clean them, so I'd just have to go in as is. *It's just you and me, womb juice!*

I parked illegally in management's driveway as 11.02 am ticked over. I sat at the steering wheel and reminded myself, *Play the part of yourself. If they don't want you, they aren't for you.* My inner prick threw up a visualisation of a publisher looking at me over a table, one eyebrow raised, gobsmacked that such a bad idea could even be presented to a professional. I whacked that and stepped out of the car. I walked three steps and looked down as a rustling came from my $25 boots . . . *Fuck, a cheeseburger wrapper from my car is stuck to my shoe!* I bent down, trying to hide my stained rear end from traffic, and stuffed the cheeseburger wrapper in my pocket.

An exceptionally trendy-looking older woman, with huge red glasses and skin-tight leggings, opened the door. 'Jess! Come in!' As she gave me a huge hug, my inner narrative screamed at me, *I bet she can smell period!* If she could, she was too polite to mention it, merely asking, 'Would you like to wait in the waiting room for Cate, or would you like to sit at the table and wait for her?' Mathematically, if I was sitting at the table, there was less chance to embarrass myself visually. So I opted to sit at the table, wait, talk, say goodbye and remain sitting until Cate left.

As I entered the meeting room, my heart sank. White walls, white table, expensive white CHAIRS! When the exceptionally trendy red-glasses lady left the room, I grabbed the scrunched-up cheeseburger wrapper from my pocket and laid it out as a towel on the chair. *Breathe, Jess, breathe. Rejection is ego, nothing comes from protecting one's ego and not achieving anything. You've always wanted to do this.*

But nobody thinks you can . . .

Stop that, Jess, that's buying into someone else's shit. This is about you and what you're going to do. We are just talking words. You're not going to die or be injured because you told someone about an idea. Breathe, quit your ego, quit your inner prick, and release.

Publisher Cate arrived and Red Glasses ushered her into the room. As Cate came towards me, I realised I'd have to stand up or look socially inept. She was young, with dark-brown hair, and approached me with the warmest smile on her face. Nothing like my inner visualisation of the woman who hated me! I stood up to greet her and quickly looked down to see if the cheeseburger wrapper was still on the seat. IT WAS GONE! We embraced in a hug and exchanged smiles, and as we disconnected from the hug, I looked behind me again. The cheeseburger wrapper was stuck to the back of my pants! In shock, I stayed standing longer than everyone else. When I finally sat, during the awkward start of the meeting when nobody was talking, I heard a scrunching sound as the layers of arse, pants, period, cheeseburger wrapper and chair made contact.

But despite all that, Cate started the meeting with, 'So, I'm excited to hear your idea. Your manager has sent me through quite a few pieces already, and I love them.' I got to go home and smash that sugar-free Vodka Cruiser after all.

✗

Once you start asking for what you want and you achieve it, it is a high that I can only imagine is as thrilling as a hit of heroin. It becomes addictive! Life is a game and I really want you to start actively playing your pieces. No, stuff it, I want you to become the bloody BANKER. You deserve it!

If you're working, how many times have you missed something really important to you because you are too scared to ask for the day off? You've missed a moment in time! Start navigating your game of life so you're playing to win. If you let fear or worry move your Monopoly pieces around the board, you aren't playing your game; you're letting your reaction to someone else's game dominate your life.

Don't put yourself down and tell yourself you're taking the easy way out by not asking for what you want in life, because that is not the easy way at all. It's actually the hardest way to live your life. I hear all the time: 'I'll wait for the kids to get older/until my next tax return/until I'm more stable, and then I will start asking for what I want in life.' Bullshit! There's never a perfect moment to be in control of your life; there's always going to be shit going on. Quit your ego. Quit your inner prick. Quit it all and just start asking the questions.

If you want to start a course, ask when it starts, ask how you can enrol, ask them what payment method they would prefer, ask them if there's a payment option, ask them to send your certificate of completion to your address, ask for a bottle of champagne at your graduation, ask someone to pass the lobster when you're out for dinner celebrating your first promotion. Congratulations! You just did that thing you've been talking about doing your entire life. You'll have some cheeseburger, womb juice, Clive moments along the way. But you'll stop being a talker and start being a doer. You'll start being an active player in your own game of life. You'll inspire your friends; you'll inspire your children. You'll start getting comments like, 'I wish I could do that,' and your natural inner response will be, *You can! You just choose not to.*

Read this chapter again before your first go at asking for what you want. Here are the main points to remember:

- You are playing a game so don't worry about the response.

- Quit your ego right now! If you start to ask for something and your inner prick says, *But what if they say no/you're an idiot, etc.*, you'll know you're being tricked due to your previous habits of not asking for what you want. Stop it, remind yourself you're actively living and not just existing anymore.

- Don't tell too many people what you're doing until you've done it. Why are you telling them? Are you seeking validation? Why do you need that validation? You're asking for what YOU want to do. Your inner narrative isn't looking for validation, it's seeking negative responses to talk yourself out of progressing.

- When loved ones highlight negatives in your desire to ask for what you want, don't engage in a debate. You're doing something they're too scared to, and they're just trying to protect you. Don't worry, you'll inspire them when things start swinging your way. You've quit that emotion of replaying all of the negatives, remember? Reply with, 'Thanks for your concern but I'm fine.' You need your energy and focus to achieve what you want in life.

Now, stop reading and start asking!

Conclusion

FAILING IS FINE!

*G*reat news! Everyone in life is a failure, so you aren't alone. Nobody is perfect (people even criticise the Dalai Lama!) so you need to stop striving for perfection and basing your existence on it. If you view yourself as a failure, ask yourself if would you view a person travelling on a similar path as a failure. NO? That's because it's harder to love ourselves then to love someone else. Anger and stress blind our logic, creating irrational narratives of ourselves. Being a failure is the go-to inner arsehole narrative that we have. True success in life is loving and valuing yourself and others. If you don't think you're worthy of loving yourself, go back to page one and read this book again.

Your fingers have been on my words for a good couple hundred pages now, so I feel we have an intimate relationship. I need to have an honest word with you. You are NOT a failure. You have goals you may not have achieved, and you have a 'should' mentality that says your life 'should' be different. But that's a comparison to a perfect world that doesn't exist, remember? The most important part is don't give up on yourself. EVER!

Practise your confidence and not your ego. Identify the source of your inner prick and practise changing the narrative. Keep an eye out for when you've boarded the arsehole train or are being a negative narcissist. Get to know your authentic self and never compromise on that. You're wonderful, unique and you're already practising fantastic things. There's something about you that nobody else has, and that's YOU. The true sadness in society is we give up on ourselves.

Remember yourself as a five-year-old. I want you to look into that five-year-old's eyes: are you willing to tell a child they aren't good enough? Because you are still that child. You still have the same heart, lungs, kidneys. You may have grown, but you are still that person. Don't give up on that child; don't give up on yourself. Don't rob yourself and the world of knowing the authentic you.

You may have been through trauma; you may have had hard times. But I'm begging you, do not give up. You deserve to love yourself. You might tell yourself you are a bad person, but you're just the product of a series of bad habits learnt as a result of your trauma, whether that be major or minor. Don't let the person who gave you that trauma win. Don't let them continue to traumatise you until your last day on earth. Take your life back, snatch it back right now unapologetically.

Don't build your self-worth on judgement; you're no better than anyone else. But also don't think anyone else is better or has permission to dominate a particular train of thought.

You're going to be okay, because you have you, glorious, fabulous, strong (even if you don't realise it) YOU! And you now know how to change the way you think and create new habits. You don't have to master it on the first go, or even the first twenty goes. But you can't give up! The only person who chooses the way your life pans out is you. If you answered, 'Yes, but . . . *insert excuse here*,' you're still lying to yourself.

You can start internalising love for YOU right now. Start the prick cleanse tomorrow, if you can, or whenever you're ready, but you can feel reassured that whenever you do start, you'll have a road map. Maybe you can get a friend to read this book, and you can practise the methods together! (This isn't a way for me to sell more books, by the way. Give them your copy of the bloody thing if you need to.) I see the sadness in incredible people's eyes; I hear their stories that they don't think they are good enough. It's like listening to Cathy Freeman telling me she's not a fast runner, or Elle Macpherson telling me she's ugly. It's incomprehensible that someone so amazing could have such little self-worth. How can one be so blind to their own fabulousness? If you do not love yourself, your inner prick is robbing you blind of the joy in life.

Look at Walt Disney. He was told by his former news-paper editor that he lacked imagination and had no good ideas. But he didn't give up, like you shouldn't. No doubt his internal narrative would have been telling him he'd never make it. But he created new habits to give himself the love and self-worth that created Disney. His take on failure was, 'I think it's important to have a good hard failure when you're young . . . Because it makes you kind of aware of what can happen to you. Because of it I've never had any fear in my whole life when we've been near collapse and all of that. I've never been afraid.'

Theodor Seuss Geisel, better known as Dr Seuss, had his first book rejected by 27 publishers. He went on to sell millions of copies worldwide. Could you imagine life without *The Cat in the Hat*? If his inner narrative had gotten the best of him, there'd be no *Green Eggs and Ham*!

Oprah Winfrey was fired from her first job as a news anchor, because she was 'unfit for TV'. If she'd let this feedback control her internal narrative, she wouldn't now be one of the richest self-made women in America. Oprah completely controls her own game these days, but she didn't start out that way.

It's hard to imagine Beyoncé ever losing at anything, but back when she was starting out, her group Girl's Tyme lost a TV talent show. Beyoncé might have decided then that she wasn't good enough to perform. But she believed in herself, and that girl group would go on to be Destiny's Child, later launching Beyoncé's successful solo career and empire.

Remember when I told you in chapter 3 that Stephen King's wife took his draft of *Carrie* out of the bin and convinced him to keep working on it? Let's role play. You're Stephen King and you've given up on your dream of writing this novel. You've throw it in the bin, surrendering to what you think is the inevitability of a life just existing. I'm Stephen King's wife, putting my hand in the bin, blowing off the breadcrumbs and handing it back to you. Don't give up, don't surrender . . . I'm begging you!

You've got this! Why wouldn't ya?

Until next time,

Jess x

Acknowledgements

Norm, Freddie, Matilda, a girl whose nickname is Flange. My gay ex-boyfriend and godfather to our daughter, Ro. My mum. My neighbour June. The guy who works at the corner shop for always making me laugh and sharing your wisdom (we have not exchanged names yet). A bloke called Botters and his wife Michelle who put up with us drinking on their back deck all the time. Our other neighbour called Patty for telling us the same jokes for three years straight. A bloke called Ronnie for sitting with us by a campfire, a girl called Mia for sitting with us on plastic chairs and drinking cheap wine. A bloke called AJ who leapt to stardom on two episodes of *Dinner Dates* in 2012 and now drinks with us at the bowls club. His wife Barcia who makes killer margaritas. Gorgeous Sunny! Our daily talks of the world and this book are better than a bottle of the finest white wine. And my gorgeous friend Laura whom I talk to everyday; together we actively practise and imagine the exercises in this book. I couldn't have done this without you.